PROGRAMME ON EDUCATIONAL

Redefining
the Place
to Learn

ORGANISATION FOR ECONOMIC CO-OPERATION AND DEVELOPMENT

ORGANISATION FOR ECONOMIC CO-OPERATION AND DEVELOPMENT

Pursuant to Article 1 of the Convention signed in Paris on 14th December 1960, and which came into force on 30th September 1961, the Organisation for Economic Co-operation and Development (OECD) shall promote policies designed:

- to achieve the highest sustainable economic growth and employment and a rising standard of living in Member countries, while maintaining financial stability, and thus to contribute to the development of the world economy;
- to contribute to sound economic expansion in Member as well as non-member countries in the process of economic development; and
- to contribute to the expansion of world trade on a multilateral, non-discriminatory basis in accordance with international obligations.

The original Member countries of the OECD are Austria, Belgium, Canada, Denmark, France, Germany, Greece, Iceland, Ireland, Italy, Luxembourg, the Netherlands, Norway, Portugal, Spain, Sweden, Switzerland, Turkey, the United Kingdom and the United States. The following countries became Members subsequently through accession at the dates indicated hereafter: Japan (28th April 1964), Finland (28th January 1969), Australia (7th June 1971), New Zealand (29th May 1973) and Mexico (18th May 1994). The Commission of the European Communities takes part in the work of the OECD (Article 13 of the OECD Convention).

Publié en français sous le titre :

UN NOUVEAU LIEU D'APPRENTISSAGE

Acknowledgments

Site visits were conducted in 14 countries to collect the information for the study, and many people were involved in meetings, tours and providing information for the research.

It would be difficult to list here everyone who participated, however in particular, I would like to thank: Ann Gorey, Brian Frankham, Nick Van Exter, Dom Valeri and John Mayfield, Australia; Beech Williamson, England; Ritva Kivi and Juoni Kuusisto, Finland; Martine Safra and Sylvain Viriot, France; Jacob Hobjerre, Denmark; Gregor Friedl, Germany; Dr. Hideki Shimizu, Nick Kajita, Fumihito Miyamoto, Mr. Akishige Hirai, Japan; Jin Bok Suk and Chang Kee Min, Korea; Willem Kleinbruinink, The Netherlands; and John Simpson, New Zealand; Laura Stevenson and Martin Garden, Scotland; and Marianne Wedin, Sweden.

It would not have been possible to have completed this project without the assistance of educators and administrators of the schools and universities which we visited who graciously took the time to show us their facilities and provide us with a great deal of information.

As well, the architects who designed the buildings highlighted in the study had an active role in the development of this document. The floor plans and a number of the photographs that appear in the guide were supplied by the architects.

Finally, I would like to acknowledge the work of the members of the NJIT-Architecture and Building Science Research team, in particular, my colleague Anton Wolfshorndl, for their dedication to this project.

Susan Stuebing
Assistant Professor for Research
New Jersey Institute of Technology

New Jersey Institute of Technology
School of Architecture
Architecture and Building Science Research

Educational Environments Research Team

Susan Stuebing,	Assistant Professor
Anton Wolfshorndl	Architectural Researcher
Leslie Knox Cousineau	Architectural Researcher
Stephanie E. DiPetrillo	Architectural Researcher

Cover

Background Image: Interior Street, Thomas Telford School, Telford, England

Top Photo: Student works at computer in Oldham Sixth Form College, Oldham, England

Bottom Left: Students collaborate on portable computers at the Methodist Ladies College (MLC), Melbourne, Australia

Bottom Right: Students at Seoul Science and Math High School work together in computer lab, Seoul, South Korea

MLC Photo provided by David Loader, all others by S. Stuebing

4

The Programme on Educational Building

PEB promotes the international exchange of ideas, information, research and experience in the field of educational facilities. For more than 20 years, it has worked to ensure that the maximum educational benefit is obtained from past and future investment, so that buildings and equipment are designed effectively as well as planned and managed efficiently.

The three main themes of the programme's work are:

● improving the quality and suitability of educational facilities and thus contributing to the quality of education;

● ensuring that the best possible use is made of the very substantial sums of money which are spent on constructing, running and maintaining educational facilities; and

● giving early warning of the impact on educational facilities of trends in education and in society as a whole.

Since man first learned to write, technology has brought about changes in the way in which knowledge and information is communicated. But the technological developments of the past few years have been so dramatic, and so rapid, that we have been unable fully to assimilate them into our educational processes. Many reports have been written about the potential of new information and communication technologies, and the effects - not all of them desirable - that they might have on the way in which learning is organised. The OECD Programme on Educational Building (PEB) published one such report in 1992.

The present study does not set out to make predictions, but to report on what is already happening in a selection of educational institutions from across the OECD area. The researcher's remit was to identify buildings where new technologies have been introduced in a deliberate way, and to report on how this has been done. The outcome is a unique survey of educational buildings in the last years of the twentieth century. The 21 case studies which make up the bulk of the report speak for themselves. The schools they describe are not in any sense models to be followed, nor do they necessarily represent all that is most advanced in the use of technology in education, but they do collectively illustrate the range of approaches that are being adopted.

The report describes in plans, photographs and words what the researcher saw. Its conclusions about the lessons which architects and managers may need to draw from these examples are given in an introductory chapter. The Programme on Educational Building is pleased to have been able to work with the New Jersey Institute of Technology in funding the preparation of this report. The publication of this report is intended to inform decision-makers and practitioners in education about what is happening, and to stimulate discussion and reflection about the future. The views expressed in it do not commit the Secretary-General of the OECD or any of its Member countries.

Table of Contents

Introduction

Throughout the past decade, educators, architects and administrators have imagined and explored how information technology might change education. New schools have been designed and existing facilities have been renovated throughout the world. These "schools of the future" represent a significant investment of thought, time and money. They reflect the vision of educators as they seek a new approach to education in which information technology becomes one of many tools for learning. This report describes 21 educational buildings where innovative use has been made of information technology in the educational process.

The report was released as a preliminary printing for the Learning Education Technology Australia Conference (LETA) in the September 1994. The study has been partially funded by the OECD Programme on Educational Building (PEB). The study represents the second phase of PEB's activity on the impact of new technology on educational buildings. The first phase was described in a report by Norman Willis.[1]

The 21 schools and educational institutions presented have been selected because - in the eyes of the researchers, or of the governments of the countries concerned - they offer experience which is felt to be of interest to educational professionals. The examples represent important concepts for integration of technology, building organization and requirements to meet changing teaching and learning methods. They should not necessarily be taken as a statement of what is best, as the case studies present a range of ideas. As buildings take two to five years to plan, design and construct, these examples do not necessarily reflect the most current equipment. Information technology continues to develop at great speed, and no compendium can hope to be exhaustive. For this reason, the study points toward the need for further research, and exchange of experience.

STUDY METHOD

This study is based on a series of site visits conducted by the author during the spring and autumn of 1993. Site visits were selected through consultation with officials in countries participating in the OECD Programme on Educational Building. Approximately 75 school buildings, higher education and auxiliary educational buildings were documented.

As well, background research (including discussions with industry) has assisted in identifying school sites and other educational settings of interest. Within the overall aim of identifying and documenting exemplary technology-rich educational facilities, the study takes a multidisciplinary approach reviewing issues in education, technology and architecture. It is a broad survey, relying heavily on information provided by the schools, and the observations of educators and administrators using them. Largely, the study is descriptive in nature.

COUNTRIES STUDIED

Australia
Canada
Denmark
Finland
France
Germany
Japan
Korea
The Netherlands
New Zealand
Sweden
United Kingdom
United States

The study has been conducted with the assistance of the ministries and departments of education in these countries.

[1] Norman Willis, *New Technology and Its Impact on Educational Buildings.* Programme on Educational Building, Organisation for Economic Co-operation and Development, Paris 1992. p. 30.

9

Interviews were conducted with educators, administrators, researchers, architects, policy makers and technology providers. The focus of these discussions was the inpact of new technologies on the design and construction of educational facilities.

Materials were gathered through these interviews and subsequent correspondence with the schools, administrators and their architects. Included were reports, architectural plans, and other descriptive materials such as brochures and journal articles. Where possible, research reports documenting the use of the facility were requested and reviewed.

NEED FOR THE STUDY

Under the right conditions and with adequate funding, the process of developing a vision for the "School of the Future" is inviting to the educator, administrator and architect, alike. A school with technology-based learning tools catches our imagination and offers hope that we will be able to provide an interesting and exciting world in which our students can learn and excel. For this reason alone, perhaps "the desire to dream" would justify a study of schools to date. However, there are other reasons why this study of successful, built examples of technology-rich schools should be useful to educators and administrators. Increasing demands on education and new opportunities with information technology require that we rethink the way we design and use educational facilities.

Increased demand for technology-based education

Educators are concerned with preparing students for living and working in societies where new information technologies will be ubiquitous. Economic and employment forecasts predict that there will be increased demand for technology-literate students today and in the future. The benefits of, and obstacles to, the use of new technology in teaching and learning have been documented. Lack of adequate teacher training or curriculum development, as well as insufficient access to appropriate software are some of these obstacles. Nevertheless, an acceleration of the use of information technology in education is apparent. National educational curricula and policy statements demonstrate that the introduction of information technology into the learning environment will continue. At the same time, technology-based education and retraining for industry reinforces the need for life-long learning.

Planning for Information Infrastructure

Planning for the technology-rich facility is a complex process. In many cases, the design process of the schools described in this study utilized a collaboration which maximized the diverse expertise of many disciplines. This exchange created a context for innovation and exploration. To support this planning process, a shared language is needed. New modes of delivery (such as networking and distance learning) and changing teaching and learning methods may call for rethinking the use and even the types of facilities which will be required in the future.

Rapid change in types and use of information technology

Information technology, as a tool for learning, is developing very rapidly. Computers are more versatile and more powerful; hardware is becoming cheaper and more portable; applications are more wide-ranging and easier to use. At the same time, educational methods are shifting, putting new demands on the use of the building. Planning and designing educational facilities requires anticipating and calculating for two very different yet convergent time frames: rapid rate of change in technology, and time to design and construct a new facility. To prepare for, and to respond to these changes, planning and design needs to incorporate flexibility and adaptability.

Specific design requirements

Educational settings which incorporate information technology have specific design requirements. They are: (1) the distribution of an information network; (2) furniture design and organization of equipment; and (3) health and safety requirements for heating, ventilation and lighting.

Cost

Several factors make future costs for educational facilities difficult to predict. These include: (1) the scale of demand for technology-based education; (2) changing demographics and labor-market needs; (3) expanded and changing curriculum requirements; and (4) the emergent nature and capabilities of information technology. Increased cost can be attributed to networking, requirements for flexibility, furnishings, lighting costs, required air conditioning and alternative ventilation systems. Costs also include equipment (hardware and software), facility maintenance, networks, technical staff and faculty training.

EXAMPLES SELECTED

The examples in this study were selected for their relevance to public policy and their potential interest to educators and administrators. A range of building types and design solutions were considered, including:

(1) pragmatic ways to construct new, or enhance existing facilities to enable greater use of information technology;

(2) alternative educational settings which seek to reorganize the school building to respond to changing educational agendas;

(3) infrastructure or delivery strategies which alter the size requirements and organization of the school facility; and

(4) the architects' and educators' vision of the school facility as a symbol of the future.

Several aspects of change in education are presented in these examples, including: new teaching and learning methods, alternative educational delivery, and changes in the population or sectors served. All are innovative, but not all are costly. Some which do involve high initial or development costs have been planned so as to defray these through long-term savings. These case studies represent a pool of information about the design, construction and use of "classrooms of the future" which may serve to inform future decisions by others.

Technology proved to be more than a catalyst for change in learning and teaching practices; it also ushered in an entirely new culture in which the school became a community of learners where co-operative and collaborative learning became the norm.[1]

Irene Grasso and
Margaret Fallshaw

Clockwise from upper left corner: (1) Older students coach younger students on multimedia project at Camden Elementary School; (2) Teacher's adopt the role of a coach at Ainsley Girls School; (3) students at Ainsley Girls School work on a school-wide solar car project; (4) At Adelaide's "School of Tomorrow" students work in teams at a day-long program to receive an introduction to information technology. All examples are from Adelaide, South Australia.

Key Indicators

Technology, Educational Change and School Buildings

Information technology is one important factor changing teaching and learning methods with significant implications for the provision, design and renovation of educational buildings. These changes are taking place in different ways, depending on national politics, institutional characteristics and personal aims. As the Willis report indicates, "The difficulty in establishing trends in education and training systems is that they vary so much from country to country. . . . The weight of history and cultural traditions lies heavily upon our educational provision. . . ."[2] Nevertheless, from the study of over 75 educational environments within 14 countries, a common set of concerns, requirements and approaches are emerging for the design of technology-rich school buildings and use of the information infrastructure.

BACKGROUND: Gradual Change in "Classroom Culture"

Much of the earliest software was aimed at the acquisition or reinforcement of basic number or language skills and these programs were still widely used during the period of the inspections. Normally they were used with younger children and frequently resulted in poor work. Too often tasks failed to challenge the children or were not relevant to other work, pupils lacked the IT skills necessary to manipulate the programs and there was too little immediate support from the teacher.[3]

"The Teaching and Learning of Information Technology"
Her Majesty's Inspectorate

Effective use of information technology continues to be a key concern of the educational community. Early theories suggested that the computer would substitute for teacher-centered instruction therefore allowing the teacher time for other activities.[4] Since these early explorations, the concept of Computer Aided Instruction (CAI) has significantly evolved, and has even been dismissed by educators. In its place, technology is viewed by many educators as a tool for learning applicable to nearly all subject areas. Student activities within the technology-rich classroom are characterized by greater interactivity, creativity and inquiry.[5] The teacher, no less than the student, has become an active learner. The teacher's role has changed out of necessity in the context of rapid introduction and advances in information technology.[6]

Studies on the educational process suggest that the use of information technology can have many benefits.[7] As cited in the recent Kings College study of primary and secondary schools in England, some of these benefits include: increased motivation, heightened enjoyment, heightened concentration, complexity of the project, pride in the product and conceptual awareness.[8]

Entrance to Lycee
Polytechnic, Vesoul, France

School as we know it is thus already paradigmatic, patterned heavily by analogies, metaphors and symbols, many of which are derived from a fairly distant past. Furthermore, the paradigm creates the tangible things about school — the way it is organized, the shape of its buildings, the nature of its ceremonies and rituals, the way the learning programme is conceived of, set out, and even taught.

H. Beare and R.Slaughter [12]

Teaching methods that make use of technology are varied and developing. The following are among those that have been encountered: (1) greater student collaboration, (2) project based work, (3) interdisciplinary study, and (4) student centered-study.[9] Information technology is also being used successfully for the delivery of lectures and distance learning.

Expanding Definition of "Classroom": A Place For Learning

". . . (Oppenheimer) cherished a vision of shared cultural stewardship, in which all the cultural agencies of the region- libraries, parks, radio and television stations, museums, and art centers would assume joint responsibility for educating the general public. . . . In contrast to classroom routines . . . museums offer the learner the opportunity to stop at will, to loiter and repeat, to ignore what does not stimulate and to share what seems interesting."[10]

Hilde Hein,
THE EXPLORATORIUM: The Museum as Laboratory

Similar to the vision for the Exploratorium in San Francisco, educators' definition of the "place to learn" is expanding beyond the classroom. Information technology can have a liberating effect in terms of the time and space within which teaching and learning takes place. This may suggest a new relationship of the school facility to its surroundings. For example, the Saturn School of Tomorrow in St. Paul, Minnesota was designed with an idea that, at any one time, one third of the students would be studying outside of the building at various local cultural centers.[11]

Arrangements such as these are increasingly popular as educators seek to reinforce the relationship between education and the work place. Students at Ainsley Girls School (Adelaide, Australia) designed and built a solar car to compete in the "Darwin to Adelaide Solar Car Race Challenge." The work on this vehicle took place in many different types of settings within and outside the school. The solar car was finally constructed by the students at a local General Motors plant. In this way, the students gained a larger perspective in many areas of study, and made a connection from their studies to industry.

Why "Schools of the Future"?

What is surprising about the schools in the 1980s is not the differences from previous generations but the similarities. We should therefore not be over-optimistic about those changes which can be expected to occur during the next generation. Most of the teachers who will be teaching at the end of this century are already teaching. Most of the schools which will be providing educational facilities are already built. . . . The architectural challenge therefore is to retrieve intelligence from obsolescence.[13]

Sam Cassels

There is no one model for a technology-rich learning environment. The "school of the future" is an evolving model. In a sense, the examples presented in this report should be thought of as "snapshots in time," not as a view of the future. Ongoing change, both in technology and educational practice continues to alter our view of the possibilities.

At the same time, there is a more fundamental question: will school facilities as we know them be required at all in the future, given the flexibility, independence and networking power of information technology?

The following text distills the findings of this study of technology-rich school buildings into four key indicators of change. However, the case studies are the critical presentation, as they present the "school of the future" as a total and integrated place for learning with new teaching methods, changing roles for students and teachers, and new use of equipment.

Keeping the need for a comprehensive design in mind, the four key indicators for the design and use of educational environments presented here include:

1. **Defining the Place for Learning:** The classroom has remained a constant for nearly a century. With information technology and new teaching and learning methods, will the classroom continue to be a uniform design? Or will new models for the "place for learning" develop? How will the design and use of these spaces differ from the classroom as we know it?

2. **Building Connections:** With the increased use of networking and the information highway, will the role of the building diminish or are there new requirements which will be placed on the facility? Will distance learning significantly affect the requirements for educational facilities? What impact will networking have on urban and rural schools?

3. **New Building Use Requirements:** Are there new use requirements which alter the way schools are designed? Who will use these facilities? Will the use of information technology expand educational building use to a larger population than the traditional school age student?

4. **Transforming Support Facilities for Learning:** The use of information technology in teaching and learning requires increased teacher support and professional development. At the same time, new materials are required such as software, videos and other multi media and data base materials. Expertise and maintenance requirements also suggest the potential needs for educational support centers. What are the requirements for these facilities?

1. DEFINING THE PLACE FOR LEARNING

The introduction of information technology has led to change in the way the nearly universal standard classroom is used. However, simply replacing the classroom with an equally universal update, including computers, networking and electronic presentation equipment, is unlikely to be possible.

The schools studied for this report include a range of learning areas and classroom types including laboratories, study spaces and resource centers. These examples suggest that there is no one type of room or building organization that serves the changing nature of educational instruction. Flexibility, adaptability, appropriate size, configuration, and ease of access to technology are the key physical design criteria. The design principles for some of these environments borrow from the concepts of the "Open Plan" of the late 60s and early 70s, now modified to meet the requirements of information technology, while other examples are actually located in open plan school facilities built during that era.

Many educators interviewed as part of this study expressed the view that the concentration of equipment in dedicated computer labs is likely to be replaced by a more integrated school-wide approach. In part, this will be the result of increasing quantity of equipment available to schools as national figures indicate, and due to reduced cost of equipment.

As the quantity of information technology increases, its organization and distribution could ensure effective use integrated with other teaching tools and methods across the curriculum. Distribution of equipment and the design of places for learning include: building-wide access (the computer lab or specialized labs or information centers); shared classroom-cluster access (technology centers and study areas); and, fully-integrated classrooms (including the use of the portable computer).

Computer Rooms

The criticism of the computer lab as neutralizing the computer is not to be taken as denying that computers in a room apart can be used in wonderful ways – so long as the room apart is allowed to become the meeting point of ideas that were previously kept separate.[14]

Seymour Pappert,
The Children's Machine

Historically, the computer room or lab has been the most common response to the use of the computer for teaching.[15] Given the expense of the technology, the computer lab has been seen as the way to ensure that all students in a school will have access to a computer within a set time frame, and also allows for full group instruction. Unfortunately, scheduling class time in the computer lab limits spontaneity of use and implies that the use of information technology is a subject area and not another tool to support learning.

Initially, design of the computer lab was patterned after a lecture format with computer workstations in rows, all facing to the front of the room. Over time, the lab concept has evolved so that it has become a place for interactive and diverse activities. Educators look toward the computer lab to allow for: (1) student collaboration; (2) project based work; (3) use of other tools, equipment (for example robotics and other control equipment), books or paper; and (4) visual connection between the computer lab and other related study areas. Increasingly, rooms within schools are being converted (or designed)

Octagonal tables are custom designed for the Oldham Sixth Form College (Oldham, England) Language Lab.

to provide extensive use of information technology in support of particular areas of the curriculum such as science, language or media studies. The mix of lab types allows for flexibility as well as meeting the needs of specific curriculum. These labs vary in size and organization depending on activity.

Shared Information Technology Areas

Many educators look toward providing students with the ability to use computers in all classrooms. One solution is the portable or lap top computer. There are a number of initiatives currently underway to explore a future in which all students will have portable computers.[16] Portable computers are seen as solving many of the problems of the use of information technology in schools by offering increased flexibility, reducing space requirements, and reducing the need for immediate access to power.

Shared technology resource areas or "mini-computer" centers have also been used to address this issue. Shared resource areas between classrooms allow for ready access to computers while maximizing the use of equipment. The resource area also helps to facilitate team teaching. The Thomas Telford School in Telford, England exemplifies this approach. Three classrooms share a "resource center" equipped with four computers, a printer and a copying machine. Existing schools have also developed shared technology areas between classrooms. For example at Kuokkala Lower Secondary Education Center in Finland, computer niches were created within the corridor space between two classrooms to allow for ease of access.

Fully Integrated Classrooms

Schools and education authorities, generally, are seeking to increase the computer-to-student ratio to enable information technology to be used more widely and frequently. Today, few schools can afford a model which provides a 1-1 ratio of computers to students within the classroom. Generally, examples of schools which integrate the computer into all classrooms are found at the primary level. However, the most common approach is to place one or two computers in each classroom for example, the Young Hoon E. School in Seoul, South Korea.

Young Hoon E. School, Seoul, South Korea. This school was a single-loaded corridor with contained classrooms that were renovated to create an open plan school. As well, the computer lab was eliminated and the computers were redistributed to allow one computer per classroom. A teacher study area is found on each floor of the school as well.

The Apple Classroom of Tomorrow, a primary school research site (a public school in California), is one example in which the ratio was increased within the typical grades one to six to approximately one computer for two students. Research on these settings indicate that with this change there is also a need: (1) for additional floor area within the room; (2) to consider the physical setting as an important component to enhance collaboration and project-based work; and (3) to offer teachers support to reorganize the typical classroom organization.[17]

Lecture Areas

Information technology has also been successfully integrated into lecture presentation areas. Many schools, such as the Lycee Pilote Innovant, in Poitiers, France, have developed a technology-based lecture setting which allows for multi media presentations with a video projector networked to computer, VCR and satellite receiver. Electronic switching devices and specially designed teacher podiums promote ease of delivery and use of many media (from computer software to satellite image or video).

2. BUILDING CONNECTIONS

It may be that there is a role (at least in the interim) for the 'electronic village hall,' or for rooms in sixth form colleges, that will provide access to the educational process for remote students without requiring the provision of expensive equipment and network access into individual homes.[18]

Brian Longhurst,
"Distance Learning Report"

Distance learning and networking access have captured many educators' imaginations due to the perceived benefits which include: improved communication; ability to deliver education to a broad educational population; accessibility; perceived cost benefits; and the possibility of extending the range and content of the curriculum of schools. Distance and open learning are not new ideas. Australia and the United Kingdom have long histories of

Distance learning
classroom at Lehigh
University, Bethlehem,
Pennsylvania, U.S.A.

distance learning, for example through the work of the School of the Air in Australia and the Open University in England.[19] School radio and TV programming by national broadcasting organizations in the UK and France have been commonplace for half a century.

Distance learning and increased use of networking introduce a range of new use, as well as organizational and technical requirements for the educational environment. Computer networks allow 24-hour access making "time independent" and "place independent" learning possible. While some have suggested that learning will become independent of the school building (or location independent), the role of the common facility for peer discussions, tutoring and other activities remains important.

The teacher-centered lecture has been the most common educational format for distance learning, supplemented by printed study units. More interactive approaches are also being explored utilizing video and audio, as well as the use of tools such as electronic marker boards, computer and the fax machine. Personal video conferencing systems allow for ease of personal exchange via the computer workstation.

Everyone agreed that there will always be a need for some defined place where people meet to learn. No-one sees the development of what one group called 'totally isolated learning'. . . . Nevertheless, there was recognition . . . that there are powerful economic and technological arguments in favour of multi-use buildings.[20]

Content

Both distance learning and networking raise the prospect of enhancing course content. Computer networks allow students and teachers to reach multiple data bases and to communicate electronically. Networking now offers access to academic libraries throughout the world. Distance learning provides for educational programing that would not otherwise be available. Educators and students can become more selective and, at the same time, customize their education.

Communication

Communication between teachers and students throughout the world is now possible via electronic mail. Networks may also enhance communication between students from diverse economic and cultural backgrounds. For example, British Telecom's Campus 2000 provides electronic mail and conferencing facilities to 200 schools (lower and upper secondary) in 11 different European countries.[21] One of the aims of this network is to "help young people to understand relationships between different cultures and traditions in their own countries and regions, and within the wider context of Europe."[22]

Learning from Home

A combination of networks and use of portable computers can potentially provide students the same accessibility to information and workstation capacity as found at school. This reinforced connection between school and home could increase parental guidance in students' education, as well as assist some students with disabilities or long-term illness.

Flexibility and School Size

It is likely, however, that rather than wholesale distance education, we will see first a hybrid approach in which students spend substantially more of their time (but not all of it) off-campus. In very crude terms, if all courses could reduce the on-campus time of a student by 50%, then the student population could be doubled with no additional building programme.[23]

Computer networks or distance learning scenarios may also reduce the required size of a school by allowing a staggered attendance schedule. Due to the increased demand for enrollment, the Thomas Telford School is considering a home learning arrangement via networking. This would allow the college to avoid a costly addition to the school and still meet the demand for enrollment. Students would attend classes at the school, as well as receive some lectures at home. This strategy could also be employed for communities in which short-term enrollments occur due to immigration or natural disaster.

While research indicates benefits of small schools, they are often vulnerable because they are costly, and because they have difficulty in offering a full range of subjects. Networking and distance learning may assist in supporting the small school with a broad range of educational curriculum, reinforcing the viability and enriching the educational content. Potential school closures due to lack of enrollment may be readdressed by supplementing educational programs with distance learning. School size is currently broadly debated between the ability to offer a diverse curriculum within a large enrollment and the positive social benefits of the small school. Distance learning and networking may become an important part of this discussion and an increased argument for supporting the small school.

Reducing Isolation in Rural Schools

In between small isolated schools . . . there is frequent networking. . . arranged either officially or by more informal means . . . . In all these cases the use of new technology, though not common at present can help overcome the isolation of the small schools. The . . . CD-ROM offers low-cost information resources which until quite recently would have been the envy of many large schools. The fax system opens up opportunities for exchanges and communication with schools elsewhere in the country, and indeed abroad.[24]

Mme Martine Safra
Ministere de l'Education Nationale, France

Networking systems and distance learning could make the local rural school more viable, give greater access to a broad range of information, and improve curriculum content. Reducing isolation and improving the rural school has important implications for the overall welfare of the rural community.

Urban Transportation Infrastructure

In addition to educational benefits, distance learning could potentially reduce requirements on transportation infrastructure and pollution from automobile traffic. The larger impact on infrastructure and urban planning is a current area of discussion and study. Many applications in utilizing home - work relationships have already been made within the corporate sector.

3. NEW USE REQUIREMENTS

As the demands of an "information-based" society become more apparent, governments are moving the education and training of their peoples higher up their list of priorities. They will call for a higher return from their investment in education and training facilities, both in terms of "level of product" and in terms of value for money.[25]

The cost of information technology in education coupled with a need to ensure effective learning has resulted in new use requirements for the traditional educational building. These new requirements have created learning environments which are diverse both in terms of the activities that take place and who is being educated.

Teacher Development

The view is taken at [Methodist Ladies' College] that the school needs to be redesigned to make it into a learning place for teachers as well as students.

David Loader[26]

The use of information technology as a tool for teaching requires teacher development and ongoing support.[27] Teacher development may take the form of inservice training, but many educators envisage a broader re-organization of the role of the teacher and of the timetable to support ongoing and peer learning within the workplace. Teachers need to be able to keep up with changes in applications and new products in addition to basic computer training. Teachers need dedicated and properly equipped space in which to prepare learning materials with the aid of computers and related equipment. This demand for training is costly and requires that schools be innovative in providing support for teachers.[28]

In part, the design and organization of physical environment can be part of a strategy to support teacher development. For example, at Stuyvesant High School in New York City, a teacher training room was provided in the new building, designed specifically to offer teachers support on computers and other equipment. While at Methodist Ladies' College in Melbourne, Australia, a teachers' work room is provided in each of the "learning suites."

Open Learning and Multi-sector Learning Centers

Many schools are expanding educational services to a larger population who want to learn independently and at their own pace. Information technology is viewed as a possible aid in this process. The Tea Tree Gully Cam-

Tea Tree Gully Campus of Torrens Valley Institute of TAFE, Adelaide, Australia.

pus of the Torrens Valley Institute of TAFE in Adelaide is an example of a post-secondary education facility which has specifically catered to independent learning. The building, which was designed to incorporate the ongoing use of information technology, includes learning suites with small resource or information centers and an open-office landscape environment for independent and collaborative student study. The spacious workstations are not assigned. The workstation areas are intended to create an environment in which students can comfortably work independently or with others.

Shared Facilities

In an effort to provide the best access to technology with limited resources, a number of schools have looked toward sharing technology resources with other schools or with the community. Willis' report describes the Golden Grove School Complex (Golden Grove, South Australia) which shares technology-based computer and science labs between three schools on the same campus (but have different administrations and ownership). The three schools share the most expensive facilities to maximize their use.

Brookdale Community College (New Jersey, USA) shares its Advanced Technology Center with the High Technology High School located on the college campus. In this way, the high school students have access to sophisticated media production facilities and are allowed to take college level technology courses. The high school was able to reduce its building size by sharing some spaces with the college.

Community Use

Expanding the use of educational facilities and the equipment to the wider community can spread the benefits of costly information technology. The useful working life of equipment, before it is superseded, can be as little as two years, and is seldom more than five. Under these circumstances, it is essential that the equipment be fully used. At the same time, the school can assist in meeting the increasing demand for "life-long learning," and for information technology-based training. New Leith Academy (Edinburgh,

Scotland), on the other hand, generally integrates community and school use with shared access through the same interior circulation spine. At Kawasaki High School (Kawasaki, Japan), the information center is open to the public for use of computers with on-line data base access and booths for watching language and other educational videos, in addition to books.

Partnerships with Industry

Industry partnerships may also result in changes in the design, use and organization of an educational building. Industry partnerships with schools may be the result of three commonly linked issues related to information technology: (1) rapid change in information technology requiring a direct mechanism for information transfer from industry to schools; (2) assurance that the curriculum meets with industry trends and workplace requirements; and (3) the expense of information technology in schools. The role of industry may include: providing equipment (often the most common); assisting in curriculum development and research; and conducting educational sessions for industry employees within the school setting.

4. TRANSFORMING SUPPORT FACILITIES FOR LEARNING

Facilities such as libraries or information centers, training centers, distance learning, and production centers will all have an increased role in educational activities with use of information technology. In some cases, they may even replace educational programs and the requirements for certain buildings.

Information Center

The activities and culture of the traditional library have changed with the use of information technology, and many have redefined it as the "information center." With access to data bases via CD ROMs, video disks and networked on-line service, the information center has a broad range of resources at its disposal. The adjacency or inclusion of computer labs with information centers allows for greater flexibility and expands the potential role of the information center.

Tilburg University (Tilburg, the Netherlands) is included as a case study in this document as an example of the "Library of the Future." The Tilburg Library includes a hierarchy of technology-based work and reference zones including networked computer terminals and other data base reference tools, as well as computer workstations for student study and projects. Within technology-based libraries, it is increasingly common to see no separation between computer area and the stacks for books and print media. The computer lab has expanded to be an important and integrated component of the information center in which resources can be accessed, and learning activities take place.

Teacher and Student Development Centers

Training centers are one way to pool expertise, and to offer centers of excellence for teacher development as well as student instruction. Teachers skilled in teaching with information technology are a resource to other teachers, but often do not have time or an opportunity to share their experiences. Technology-based development centers can offer an environment for learning about information technology, and exchange new ideas about teaching methods. Training centers are particularly appropriate given the rapid change in hardware and software and the increasing range of information available. The Technology Information Center (TIC) in Copenhagen, Denmark trains unemployed workers for a period of eight months as well as providing open services to the community and offers in-service training to teachers.

Production Facilities

The production facility for learning materials will also be more common in the future. Production facilities may be responsible for developing video tapes, television programs, multi media displays and software. This is not a new concept; the Landesbildstelle in Berlin, Germany has been in operation since the 1950s providing similar production services. However, the production center has become more technology-based and requires an increasingly technically qualified staff. The Open Training and Education Network's (OTEN) Strathfield building (New South Wales, Australia) which is also the headquarters for OTEN is one example of such a center. The demand for such centers is largely due to the complexity of the technology and the cost for the technology. One argument for central production of materials is to create a center of excellence with potential for academic exchange. However, as costs of equipment decrease, there is increasing argument for decentralization of production of such materials.

CONCLUSION: Criticisms and Concerns

Moves towards a technology-rich learning environment are not without criticism, nor are the "schools of the future." The main concerns raised in the course of this study are relevance, social effect, cost, inadequate teacher training, and health issues. These concerns are not an exhaustive list. The following, therefore, may be considered the beginning of the critique.

Relevance

Is a technology-rich school which is considered a demonstration, symbol or model, relevant to schools throughout a region? Or throughout the world? The perceived "over-emphasis" on information technology as an all-purpose solution to educational concerns has been debated at length over the past thirty years, even in the wake of enthusiasm and initiative on the part of educators. For many, however, technology has become synonymous with the future of education, particularly as many perceive society and the workplace shifting toward a more technology-intensive environment. Overall organization, culture and values of the school are overarching concerns for the future of education.

Social

Several administrators and educators raised concern with "obsessiveness" with regard to information technology which reflected "anti-social" behavior. This observation was coupled with concern that student use of information technology needed to be kept "in check." Similar concerns have been raised with regard to video games.[29] On the other hand, observation and research suggests that the technology-rich learning environment can be organized as a social environment, in which spontaneous cooperative learning and peer tutoring is encouraged.[30]

Technology room in Oldham Sixth Form College in Oldham, England is designed for ease of access to all students.

Accessibility

Many advances have been made to make information technology accessible to everyone. In particular, the development of "assistive technology" suggests improvements in access to information and education for the physically disabled, sight, hearing impaired and learning disabled.[31]

The need to insure accessibility regardless of economic status is a key issue raised in the Willis report. In addition to access regardless of physical ability, equal access within the educational sector and society in general continues to be of great concern.[32]

Need for Professional Development

The technology-rich facility is only one part of the overall educational system. Teacher preparation and development has been cited by many studies as being the key factor in effective integration of information technology in teaching. Yet, teacher support remains an unmet need.[33] Trade-offs between equipment, facility and staff requirements often create a paradox. A school may choose to provide information technology within the classroom, but not be able to afford the necessary teacher training to support its use. Most educators expressed concern that a successful new technology-based school or educational program should be coupled with teacher in-service training as an ongoing process.

Equipment Provision

Providing information technology to schools is a significant investment and should be an important aspect of the facility plan. Again, the emergent nature of technology puts administrators at a disadvantage in planning to provide students and teachers with access to the most up-to-date equipment. Generally equipment and software needs to be considered an operating expense which will allow for renewal of an annual percentage of the equipment. Many strategies for purchasing or leasing equipment are being explored by administrators. A key factor is the responsibility for on-going maintenance and warranty of the equipment.

Health and Safety Issues

Several health concerns, including eye strain, ergonomic questions (body posture, resulting body strain and small repetitive motion syndromes) and radiation have been expressed with regard to the use of information technology in education. Studies in these areas have been conducted within the academic community, industry and government. While many of the issues, particularly with regard to ergonomic issues, are being solved in the work place, these issues continue to remain unaddressed in many educational settings. It should be noted that not all furnishings shown in the photos in this report are ergonomically correct or recommended by the author.

FOOTNOTES

[1] Grasso, Irene, and Margaret Fallshaw, eds. *Reflections of a Leaning Community: Views on the Introduction of Laptops at MLC*, (Victoria, Australia: Ladies' Methodist College), 1993, p. 5.

[2] Willis, Norman, "New Technologies and Its Impact on Educational Buildings," Paris: Programme on Educational Buildings, Organisation for Economic Co-operation and Development, 1992 p. 25.

[3] *The Teaching and Learning of Information Technology*, London: Department of Education and Science, 1991.

[4] Cuban, Larry, *Teachers and Machines: The Classroom Use of Technology Since 1920,* New York: Teachers' College Press, Columbia University, 1988.

[5] Kazuhiko Nakayama, "How to Maintain Human Interaction and Individualized Learning in a Large Classroom with Microcomputer - Based CAI," Educational Executive Conference, Singapore, 17-19 August 1988.

[6] Dwyer, D., C Ringstaff, and J. Sandholtz, *Trading Places: When Teachers Utilize Students' Expertise in Technology -Intensive Classrooms,* paper presented at the annual meeting of the American Educational Research Association, Chicago, 1991.

[7] Sheingold, Karen, *Restructuring for Learning With Technology*, Center for Technology in Education and the National Center on Education and the Economy. See "Restructuring for Learning with Technology: The Potential for Synergy," p. 9-25.

[8] Watson, Deryn, *The Impact Summary: An Evaluation of the Impact of Information Technology on Children's Achievements in Primary and Secondary Schools*, London: Department for Education, Kings College, 1993.

[9] *The Teaching and Learning of Information Technology*, London: Department of Education and Science, 1991.

[10] Hein, Hilde,*The Exploratorium:The Museum as Laboratory*, Smithsonian Institution Press, Washington, D.C., 1990, p. 125-26.

[11] Stuebing, S, *School Design Notebook*, New Jersey Institute of Technology, Newark, New Jersey, 1992, Case Study 16.

[12] Beare, H. and R. Slaughter, *Education for the Twenty-first Century*, London: Routledge, 1993, p. 88.

13 Cassels, Sam, "Intelligent Schools" presentation at PEB-OECD Seminar, 1991.

[14] Pappert, Seymour, *The Children's Machine: Rethinking School in the Age of the Computer*, New York: Basic Books, 1992, p. 53.

15 *Computer Rooms: Making Room for Information Technology*, Glasgow: Scottish Educational Department, 1982.

16 Turnbull, Graham, "The Laptop Project: Interim Report," Glasgow: The Scottish Council for Educational Technolog, 1991. "Portables: Choosing and Using Portable Computers," Coventry: National Council for Educational Technologuy, 1992. "Portables: Portable Computers in Initial Teacher Education," Coventry: National Council for Educational Technology, 1993.

17 Stuebing, S, L. Cousineau, and J. Giddings, *Technology-Rich Learning Environments in Elementary and Secondary Schools: An Interactive Study of Physical Settings and Educational Change*, paper presented at the American Educational Researchers Association, San Francisco, 1992.

18 Longhurst, Brian, "Distance Learning Report of a Phase I Study," Salford University, British Telecom, 1992, p. 19.

19 Moyal, Ann Mozley, *Clear Across Australia.: A History of Telecommunications*, Melbourne, Victoria: Nelson, 1984.

20 Willis, p. 40.

21 Known as the European Studies Project until 1992.

22 Fayes, James, "Brief on Campus 2000," European Studies Program, Ulster Folk and Transport Museum, North Ireland.

23 Longhurst, p. 22.

24 *PEB Exchange*, No 21, Paris: OECD, February 1994.

25 Willis.

26 Grasso.

27 Dwyer.

28 Pelgrum, William and Tjeerd Plomp, *The Use of Computers in Education Worldwide*, IEA, Oxford: Pergamon Press, 1991. Also, William Pelgrum, I.A.M. Janssen Reine and Tjeerd Plomp, *Schools, Teachers, Students and Computers: A Cross-National Perspective, International Association for the Evaluation of Educational Achievement, 1993.*

29 In Germany, legislation was proposed in 1993 to restrict children under a certain age from playing video games. Legislators asserted that the video games were both violent and addictive, *Herald Tribune*, June 1993.

30 Sheingold, p. 9-25. Also, Dwyer, David, C. Ringstaff. and J. Dandhotlz, *The Evolution of Teachers' Instructional Beliefs and Practices in High-Access-to-Technology Classrooms*, paper presented at the annual meeting of the American Educational Research Association, Boston, MA, 1990.

31 Enders, Alexandra and Marian Hall, Eds., *The Assistive Technology Source Book*, Washington, D.C. Resna Press, 1990.

32 Schement, Jorge Reina, *Beyond Universal Service: Characteristics of Americans without Telephones, 1980-1993, Communications Policy Working Paper 1*, Benton Foundation, Washington, D.C., 1994. *Universal Service and the Information Highway, Communications Policy Briefing 1*, Benton Foundation, Washington, D.C., 1994.

33 Pelgrum.

APPENDIX

Background PEB-OECD Preliminary Report 1991

(WILLIS REPORT)

The starting point for this study was a report developed by Norman Willis for the OECD Programme on Educational Building entitled *New Technology and Its Impact on Educational Buildings*. In the context of expected trends in society, technology and education, the Willis report provides an overview of the design and construction of educational facilities. It identifies areas of change in education, and discusses the implications of information technologies for educational buildings over a 15-20 year time span. The conclusions from the Willis Report are summarized here.

The Interface Between Technology, Education and Society

- Information technology needs to be distributed equitably so that no sections of the community are disadvantaged physically or economically.

- Information technology will require ongoing education in the work place and in society.

- New technology could help to retain a full standard of life in rural communities.

- Individuals will assume greater responsibility for learning.

- "Fashion" could lead to decision making which was not based in educational practice.

- The potential for manipulation of students via information technology should be monitored.

Changes within the Structures and Methods of Education

- The importance of the social context of the "school" and the role of the teacher will continue. However, the nature of these roles may change.

- Information technology will enable autonomous learning.

- Teachers will need to work more closely and more collaboratively with colleagues and professionals from other disciplines.

- Teacher training will be an increased requirement.

- Two visions were seen as the role of the school in the community: (1) a social and cultural centre for the community, and (2) a community learning facility for practical access to learning.

Changes In Educational Buildings

- Buildings need to be flexible to accommodate the rapid pace of technological change.

- The educational setting should include the following characteristics: a welcoming atmosphere, facilitate new learning methods and extend "openness" to the community.

- More space is required for facilities such as library/resource areas and instructional areas.

- Communication requirements (networking) must be considered at the start of building design.

- Evaluation cost and the cost-effectiveness of learning with technology remains a problem.

- Building budgets should not ignore budgets for ongoing maintenance of buildings and technology.

- Schools should be part of a wider community resource. The use of new technology would allow the whole community to have easy access to knowledge and training.

CASE STUDIES

People within our society and culture live in an information society. . . . Many of the roots of education are entrenched in an agrarian and industrial society. Just as business has undergone massive change to remain competitive, so must education. Although the sole purpose of education should not be to prepare students for the workplace, it should be an essential goal of every school and educational system.

Gerry Smith, Principal
River Oaks Public School

Above right: Students often work in small groups with informal instructions from their teacher.

Above left: River Oaks Public School's "internal street" is a pleasant, light-filled space that functions as a meeting place and includes study alcoves.

Right: The main entrance to River Oaks Public School.

River Oaks Public School

Oakville, Ontario, Canada

River Oaks Public School is a newly built elementary school for 650 students age 6-13. Oakville, a town of 70,000 people, is a short distance west of Toronto. River Oaks was planned as a part of a district-wide effort to institute educational change. Education at River Oaks encourages students to become active learners, taking responsibility for their studies, just as they will be expected to do when they enter working life.

A new curriculum is the keystone in a series of measures being taken by the school district. At River Oaks, the design of the building, the organization of the school day, the use of information technology and staffing arrangements are all based upon the priorities established in the new curriculum. It should be noted that curriculum restructuring is an ongoing process. As one teacher stated, "The only constant at River Oaks is change – and if this was not the case, there would be something wrong."[1]

Higher education plays an important role in the process. Researchers from the education departments at University of Toronto and York University are studying the effects of the introduction of computer technology at River Oaks. These studies include classroom observation and evaluation, as well as the design of diagnostic tools. Objective evaluation is a critical component in successful restructuring, and in this way researchers are documenting the changes taking place at River Oaks, evaluating their success and progress.[2]

CURRICULUM

The new curriculum focuses on four skill components which are articulated through three main strands of instruction: human relationships, science and technology, and global awareness. A series of themes have been developed for each of the three strands at each grade level, and each theme has an associated set of language and math skills. The four skill components are:

Literacy, which includes language proficiency and numeracy as well as a basic "literacy" in the areas of science and technology, economics and "the media."

Life Skills, which comprises social skills such as conflict resolution and the ability to work collaboratively, personal organization skills such as time management and goal setting, and character issues such as leadership and rejection.

Arts, which focuses on communication in a variety of forms including music, visual arts, drama, physical education, family studies, design, and the use of information technology.

Creative Applications, which is designed to develop the ability to pursue self-directed inquiry. Students develop projects individually, in pairs, or in groups in coordination with their instructors. The focus of the project relates to the unit of study being taught at the time, and students develop a project

New Construction
K-8
Occupied September 1990
650 students

Architect:
Mekinda Snyder Partnership
Inc. Architects • Planners

The "internal street" is at its widest point directly opposite the resource center where it provides a plaza-like space and becomes a focus of activity.

plan in order to carry through the project successfully. In this way, their work is organized much the way work projects are approached in a "real-life" working scenario.

The curriculum attempts to provide students with the knowledge, skills and behaviors that will allow them to access, manage, process and communicate information. Symbolic of this change, students are even referred to as "knowledge workers."

The School Day

There is no formal timetable. Students report to "work" in the morning with their teacher. Students work primarily in their homeroom and use other areas, such the resource center and the arts facilities, as necessary. Transitions between activities are determined by the teacher and students. Teachers blend theory and practice within the classroom, finding a balance between formal class instruction and individual instruction. As teachers guide students individually in their work, they are better able to assist them when difficulties arise.

Staffing Considerations

An important decision at River Oaks is that teachers should work with the same group of students for three-year cycles. Students will stay with the same teacher as they progress from the first to the third grades, from the fourth to the sixth grades and from the seventh to the ninth grades. In this last cycle, the teacher will transfer with the students for the first year of secondary school providing continuity and helping students to make the adjustment to the new school.

At River Oaks, staff training is viewed as essential to the success of the restructured curriculum and for the effective use of technology. The staff participates in curriculum development as an ongoing process both during and after school time. All teachers were given a computer before the school opened to develop their own literacy and explore available software.

Certain teachers are designated as technology coaches. These teachers are given a small amount of time as a part of their regular duties to work with other teachers in their classrooms to implement the integration of technol-

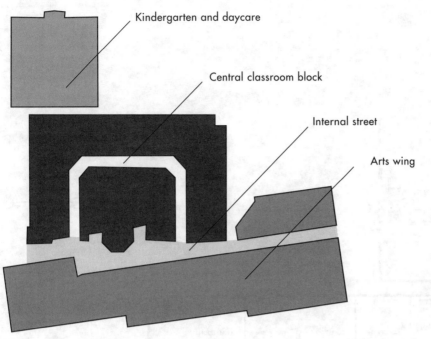

Kindergarten and daycare

Central classroom block

Internal street

Arts wing

Plan Diagram

ogy within the curriculum. This "on-the-job-training" is seen as being very effective. The idea of coaching is also extended to the students. Older students coach younger ones in the use of certain programs and equipment; for example, a second grade student may coach a kindergarten student.

BUILDING DESIGN

The school building has been specifically designed to support the restructured curriculum. This requires students and teachers to be able to move easily between homerooms and the other, specialized facilities. This has been accomplished by the organization of the classrooms adjacent to the central core of support areas, primarily the resource center.

The resource center is the focus around which all other elements are organized including classrooms, administrative areas, and the "internal street," which provides the main public space. This orientation energizes the center of the building where many resources, including multimedia computer technology, are located.

The school comprises three main blocks. The two-story central block includes the resource center, classrooms and administrative offices. The arts wing holds the art room, music room, family studies, industrial arts, gymnasium and student concourse. The third block houses the kindergarten and the childcare area.

Internal Street

The internal street is a two-story space that runs between the central block and the arts wing. It widens toward the front of the school, with the widest point at the entrance to the resource center, creating a small plaza-like space. The street/plaza concept is reinforced by the use of street lights and benches. Clerestory windows provide natural light. The street provides a

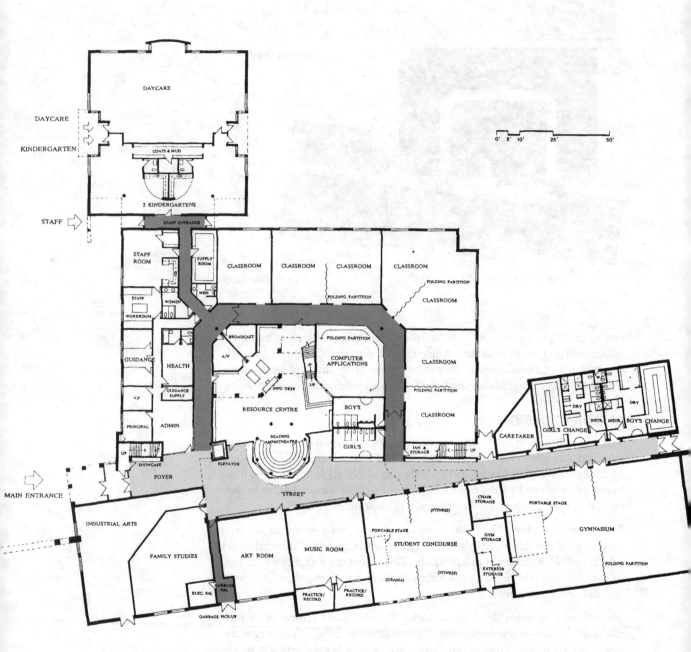

Ground Floor Plan

place for students to gather during the school day and is used for community purposes out of school hours.

Resource Center

The double-height resource center is the core of the school. A stair within the center provides direct access to the classrooms on the second floor. A major feature is the reading amphitheater with glazing to the internal street that provides an open, inviting image and introduces natural light. Multimedia computer equipment located in the resource center is a main focus of activity. The center also holds audio-visual and broadcast studios for the development of more sophisticated media projects.

The resource center is the focus of the school, providing meeting and working space for students and staff.

Classrooms

The classrooms are designed for flexible use and are placed adjacent to the key support areas in the school. All classrooms are arranged around the resource center, on two floors. There are 14 classrooms in addition to a science lab and a special education classroom. Most of the classrooms are fitted with folding partitions that allow two classrooms to be combined to form one larger space.

Three classrooms occupy the areas initially designated as computer applications rooms (one on the ground floor and two on the floor above). Once the decision was made to distribute the computers throughout the school, computer labs were no longer necessary. These rooms are designed with sliding glass partitions which allow for acoustic separation when needed, while maintaining a visual connection between the classrooms, corridor and the technology area.

Detail: second floor plan. The classroom organization forms groupings of four to six classrooms around the center core. The computer applications areas were converted to classrooms when the computers were distributed in the school.

INFORMATION TECHNOLOGY

Gerry Smith, the principal of River Oaks, firmly believes that technology should not dictate the curriculum, but rather become a seamless part of it. "If we restructured the curriculum to include the concept of information, we will not have to worry about how the technology fits. This is in fact what happened. . . . Technology has become almost transparent in the learning process for students and teachers. It is a tool for learning almost like a pencil and is used by the student or teacher when it will help them be more efficient, productive or creative. It was my experience in a previous setting.. . . that technology was layered on top of everything else. There was an attempt to force technology into the curriculum. It never found its natural place. Curriculum restructuring at River Oaks was essential to the natural inclusion of the technology in the learning process."[3]

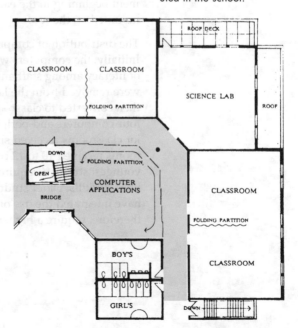

Students have access to computers in their home classrooms.

The River Oaks school building is equipped with an ethernet local area network. The network is configured with two hubs, one on each of the two stories with file servers located in the computer applications areas. Each room in the building has a minimum of five network jacks located both in the floor and in the walls. Certain rooms, such as the resource center and the computer applications areas are fitted with more connections. Each network jack can support five computers. In this way each classroom can support up to 25 computers.

There are approximately 240 Macintosh computers in the school, providing an overall computer-to-student ratio of about 1-to-3. In addition, there are scanners, CD-ROM players, video disk players, electronic keyboards, tele-communications equipment and robotics equipment. The curriculum adopts a multimedia approach in which all students learn to use this equipment beginning in the early grades. The building has a satellite dish mounted on the roof.

The distribution of computers in the school has followed a two-part policy. Initially, the computers were centralized in labs to establish a functional level of literacy among staff and students. After the second year, the computers were removed from the labs and reallocated to classrooms. The labs were then converted to classrooms. The primary grade classrooms each received four computers and peripheral equipment (scanner, CD-ROM player). Junior classrooms received six or seven computers each, and intermediate classrooms received 10 to 12 computers. The rationale for this was that the youngest students require fewer computers as they develop basic computer literacy skills. Older students have greater facility with the technology and have integrated the use of computers into their work more completely and therefore, require a higher computer-to-student ratio.

KEY POINTS

- Comprehensive curriculum restructuring was the starting point for wider educational reform.

- Technology-rich school building designed to support curriculum restructuring.

- School building is organized around the centrally located resource center.

- Internal "street" provides public space for students and community to gather.

- Classrooms organized in relation to central core of support spaces.

REFERENCES

[1] Smith, Gerry, "Restructuring Education at River Oaks P.S.: A Vision for the Future," Draft paper, June 1993: p. 1.11.

[2] The Centre for the Study of Computers in Education at York University has published a series of reports and summaries detailing the observations and conclusions of the research that has been conducted at River Oaks and elsewhere within the Halton Board of Education. These reports are available from the Centre at 4700 Keele Street, North York, Ontario, M3J 1P3 Canada.

[3] Smith, p. 1.6.

Above: aerial view shows
the urban neighborhood
in which the school is
located.

Right (top and middle):
behind the ceremonial
staircase library "corners"
provide space for students
to read and work.

Right: the lower level
entrance provides
community access to the
Social Education Center.

Ueno Elementary School

Taito-ku, Tokyo, Japan

The Ueno Elementary School is a community-based school designed with open classroom suites to provide a flexible and accessible technology-rich learning environment. This design supports cooperative learning (students working together in teams) and furnishes ancillary space that allows for the use of information technology. The open space planning is found throughout the building, including the school's library and multipurpose hall. Other, more conventional learning spaces include computer classrooms designated for both student and community use.

The school is located in a dense, urban neighborhood near the center of Tokyo and serves as a community center for the neighborhood. The social educational center provides continuing education programs for its residents. Ueno is part of a national effort to encourage "lifelong learning" put forth by the Ministry of Education, Science and Culture. The school has extensive recreational and other extracurricular facilities for its students and for the residents of the community.

BUILDING DESIGN

The school's location near the center of Tokyo poses particular constraints upon the building's site strategy. The building footprint occupies nearly the entire site. The detailing and design of the reinforced concrete structure is intended to reference traditional timber construction commonly found in Japan. The entrance sequence, exterior gardens and the massing of the building suggest a small village street.

The building is designed in two parts: (1) the classrooms and other learning spaces, and (2) the playing field, athletics facilities and community use areas. The five-story northern section of the building houses the library, a multipurpose hall with an art gallery and the school's open classroom suites. The two-story section houses the administrative offices, recreation, art and music departments and recreation facilities. A public plaza and playground are located to the south of the entire complex. A ceremonial stair leads from the public plaza to the playing field located on the roof-top of the building's southern section. The entry plaza for the school and an outdoor display area is located between the two parts of the building.

Student and faculty have access to information technology in three locations within the school, at computer labs (located on the school's ground floor), within the library, as well as within the classroom suites. Computer labs allow for a one to one relationship of students to computer; while 3-4 computers are shared within the classroom for small group instruction and individual use.

Primary School New Construction
Occupied: 1991
Architect: Shozo Uchii, Professor, School of Architecture, Kyoto University
Enrollment: 321
Building area: 10,667 m²
Cost: Y3 886 970 000

41

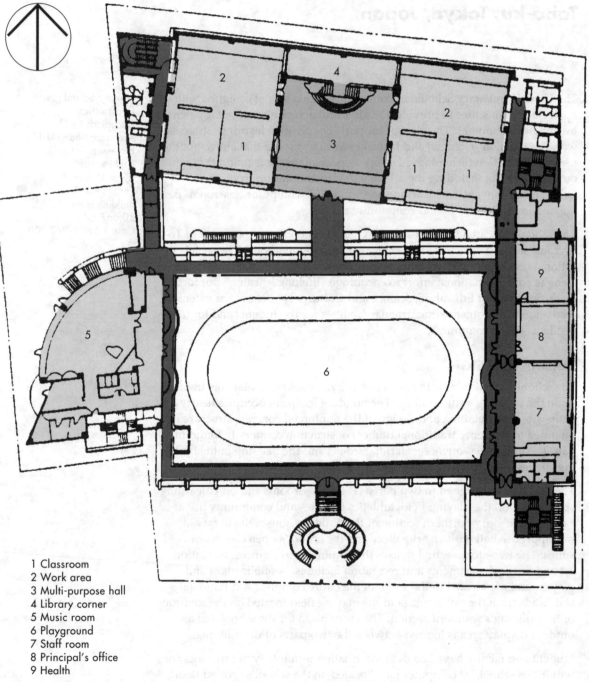

1 Classroom
2 Work area
3 Multi-purpose hall
4 Library corner
5 Music room
6 Playground
7 Staff room
8 Principal's office
9 Health

Open Classroom Suite

The open classroom suites provide an adaptable educational setting to allow for different types of learning activities including the use of information technology. There are two open classroom suites on each floor of the northern section of the building. Each suite includes two classrooms and an adjoining activity space. This space allows for student-directed learning, project work and group work. Networked computers are located in the activity space. Conduits for the network are provided in the suite design in three ways: (1) under floor channels, (2) overhead cable trays and (3) wall-mounted trunking. In addition, every classroom in the school is equipped with a ceiling-mounted television monitor, an overhead projector and a projection screen.

Classrooms are designed in open suites.

Demountable room partitions and movable furnishing units define each classroom and allow the suite to be easily re-configured to combine classrooms and to expand or contract the size of the classroom. A grid of ceiling mounted tracks allow the suite to be subdivided in several ways. These tracks are found at regular intervals and form a ceiling grid. The suite's configuration can easily be changed by moving the room partitions to another location in the ceiling grid. Half-height movable storage units separate the classrooms from the activity space, and can also be used to reorganized the classroom suite.

Multipurpose Area

The multipurpose area, the focal point of the educational wing, is located between the open classroom suites on the second and third level. The area includes three elements: the multipurpose hall, the school library and the art gallery. The double-height multipurpose hall serves as the main gathering place for the school. The library is situated behind the main stairway adjacent to the multipurpose hall and the classroom suites. The school's art gallery is located on a third floor balcony and overlooks the multipurpose hall.

Semi-open classroom suites adjoin a shared extended learning areas that include information technology resources.

Right and below:
Ueno Elementary School
provides a variety of
learning areas to
accommodate individual,
small group and whole
class situations.

TEACHING AND LEARNING

The school favors two educational approaches: student-directed learning
and team teaching. The school promotes student investigation by making
computers available at all times, both in the activity spaces and throughout
the school. The close proximity of the combination library, multipurpose
hall and art gallery to the classroom suite encourages their use for individual and group learning. Team teaching enables teachers to focus on a
particular part of the curriculum or particular aspect of information technology use. Teachers are available to provide assistance to students as well as
other teachers in their use of information technology.

Among the facilites available for public use is the swimming pool.

COMMUNITY USE

A recent initiative by the Ministry of Education, Science and Culture encourages school facilities to provide services for neighborhood use and supports "lifelong learning." This effort is intended to improve the quality of life for Japanese citizens through continuing education and extended learning.

The school is designed to be a social education center for the community. An outdoor display area enlivens the public entrance to the school and encourages people to use the school's facilities. Adult users of the facility can participate in both educational and recreational activities. These facilities are provided for adult use and student use. Educational facilities include: the computer lab, the cooking classroom, the music performance space and the music classroom. The recreation facilities include a gymnasium and a swimming pool.

KEY POINTS

- The school's design makes effective use of a tight urban site and relates contextually to its location in the center of Tokyo.

- The open classroom design provides space for group work and independent learning for students.

- The classroom suite is designed to be easily re-configured with movable furnishings for short term change and demountable partitions and ceiling grid system for long term re-organization of the suite.

- Access to info technology is provided within the classroom, in centrally located computer labs and in the school library.

- The building complex is designed to meet both student and community needs.

- It serves as a community center for its inner city neighborhood and is part of a national program to lifelong learning and recreation.

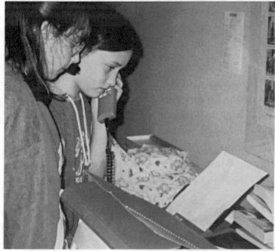

In all these cases the use of new technology, though not common at present can help overcome the isolation of the small schools. . . . CD-ROM offers low-cost information resources which until quite recently would have been the envy of many large schools. The fax system opens up opportunities for exchanges and communication with schools elsewhere in the country and indeed abroad.

Mme. Martine Safra
Ministere de l'Education Nationale, France

Above right: Small rural elementary school has approximately 60 students.

Above left: Students send fax to students at neighboring school.

Right: The entire class participates in communicating via the facsimile machine.

Facsimile and Video Text Network for Rural Elementary Schools

Vesoul, France

Isolation is one of the key concerns of the small rural school and its community. These schools may have a very small enrollment with high administrative costs and facility costs. Teaching staff may lack regular contacts with fellow professionals. Providing a broad range of educational programs and high quality educational curriculum may be difficult. While consolidation of several small schools to form a larger regional school is often seen as the solution to these problems, there are numerous disadvantages including lengthy travel for students, as well as the loss of the local "schoolhouse."[1]

The existence of a school is one indicator of the overall viability of the rural community. The closing of the local school for whatever reason may signal a decline in the community's population. Families with young children are more likely to choose to live in communities with a local school, especially a primary school. Closing the local school to assure the students receive an appropriate education, or keeping it open in the interests of the community presents a dilemma. One sees the rural school as one way to keep the rural community vital, the other focuses more on the children's development. The extended use of information technology for communication and access to data, may offer a way to avoid this apparent conflict.

FACSIMILE AND NETWORK COMMUNICATIONS

In a rural region of France, two types of technology were introduced to increase communication, reduce isolation, and offer a variety of services both administrative and educational. The use of facsimile machines, and the use of the "Minitel" system, France's nationally available video text service, were introduced to several primary schools within the Vesoul Region. Both of these technologies were well-known and simple to operate by teachers and administrators, alike. The results of the program were a success and suggest broader implications for the small rural school.

Networked Minitel, Video Text System

Facsimile machines were made available to 13 primary schools at a low cost by France Telecom. These machines were used as educational tools for students to gather information on their region and communicate with other students. The ability to communicate and to request information from other schools allowed students to broaden their perspective of their region and in a sense, to expand their educational environment.

Students learn computer applications, as well, which can be incorporated into project based work, such as the development of the student journal.

The use of the facsimile machine was coupled with the use of other forms of technology, in particular the computer for word processing and desk top publishing. Learning with these tools took place on many levels. In addition to becoming familiar with the use of technology, one product of the use of the fax was an ongoing school journal. In this way, a school with as few students as 60 students could broaden their understanding by communicating with other students in their region; report on what they had learned; and communicate this learning with other students in their region.

Network Communication

In addition, the Minitel system, a national video text system originally developed as a substitute for the telephone directory, was used as a network to support a variety of school functions and to enhance communication within the region. Some of the applications include a bulletin board for exchange between students, and for daily announcements. A poetry sharing bulletin board encouraged students to be creative and share their thoughts, while they maintained anonymity.

The network and the facsimile machine were also used administratively to reduce paperwork. The goal of the regional administrators was to develop a paper-less administration to reduce time spent on responding to forms and requests. The goal was to provide all teachers in the region with access to the network for these purposes.

SCHOOL BUILDING IMPLICATIONS

While the use of facsimile machines and a communication network may appear to be an uncomplicated interface with the rural school, the implications for school building may imply significant change in policy toward rural schools. By altering potential access to information and expanding communication, the range of the educational program and quality of teaching can be improved. At the same time, teachers, administrators and students alike, will benefit from a sense of being part of a larger educational community. The technology-rich local school could also be used for extended learning to the rural community and make available access to data bases and other resources increasing the efficiency of the school building and equipment.

In this way, the use of information technology could reduce the likelihood of closure of the rural school and in turn, strengthen the viability of the local community. At the same time, savings could be realized by reducing costs of transportation and eliminating requirements for new capital facilities costs. Through the "distance administration," it may also be possible to reduce administrative costs.

POTENTIAL MODEL

This is one example of how technology can help to reduce distances within rural areas and may help to promote the continuation of the small local school. These uses of technology could be expanded to suggest a new model for education and the rural community. Some of the features of this program which contribute to its success include: (1) simplicity and accessibility of the proposed technology (most were already familiar with facsimile machines and the Minitel); (2) redundant systems (facsimile and the network were able to achieve many of the same goals by different means); (3) low cost; and (4) access to equipment by all participating schools, teachers and administrators.

Perhaps the most interesting aspect of this approach is the simplicity of the interface and the level of acceptance. The most convincing aspect of these programs is the ease with which the students use the equipment and their excitement. The overall impact has yet to be evaluated in terms of quality of the education, staff tenure, and shifts in building and planning requirements. From the initial approach, however, the use of the technology and the results appears to be a success at a low cost.

KEY POINTS

- Information technology can assist in making small rural schools more viable through increased communication and greater access to educational resources.

- Communication through networks and facsimile machines helps to reduce isolation in rural schools, and increases the students' and teachers' links with others.

- The local rural school is often considered a key to the continued growth and life of a rural community and therefore is important to preserve; information technology may offer one important means to achieve this goal.

REFERENCES

- Safra, Martine. "The Educational Infrastructure in Rural Areas." PEB Exchange, OECD, Paris, 1994.

In the Kuokkala lower secondary school project the main aim has been to plan and construct 'school for the future' both in terms of facilities and equipment. The pedagogical aim has been to develop a good environment for students' self-directed learning using modern facilities of information technology.

Sauli Rask, Principal
Kuokkala School

Above: Non-directional furniture was designed to allow for many types of educational activities within the classroom.

Right: School exterior (nearly completed).

Below: A perspective drawing of the school.

Kuokkala Lower Secondary Education Center
Jyväskylä, Finland

The goal for the planning team for the Kuokkala Lower Secondary Education Center was to develop "the modern school." The resulting building design unites two key themes which concern our future: (1) respect for the natural environment; and (2) the increased use of information technology. These themes are combined with a new role for teachers and greater student autonomy. Information technology has an important role in promoting independent acquisition of knowledge and an "open" learning environment. The building has been designed as a total learning environment with a central street with displays to stimulate student interest, an "eco-park" on the schools grounds and a "green house" located within the center of the building. Kuokkala is included in this report as one of the few examples which was in construction during the research period.

The planning process for the building design took two and a half years, ending January in 1992. It involved experts from many disciplines including the future principal of the school, researchers from the University of Jyväskylä and experts representing fourteen curriculum areas. The committee agreed to seven principles for the design of the "modern school" including: (1) ease in understanding the building organization; (2) functionality; (3) flexibility and adaptability; (4) impact on the motivation of students; (5) natural lighting; (6) security; and (7) anticipation of future needs.

New Construction
To be completed: Spring 1994

Architect:
Arkkitehtitoimisto Kauko Lahti

13-16 age group

Number of students: 400
Number of faculty: 50

EDUCATIONAL APPROACH

The planners viewed autonomous school work as the basis for an "open" school plan. In this proposed environment, students would have more freedom of movement than within the traditional classroom. Individual subjects of study would overlap and complement one other rather than be held separate. Planners envisioned that students would take more responsibility for the course of their learning working individually and cooperatively with other students, while, teachers would have a new role to serve as a "guide." To accomplish this vision, new pedagogical practices would need to be adopted. As well, ideas of how to make such a new school work would need to be explored. Communication was viewed as a key element. Dialogue between students and teachers should increase within this proposed educational context and through the use of information technology. To allow for these changes, the school schedule needed to become more flexible.

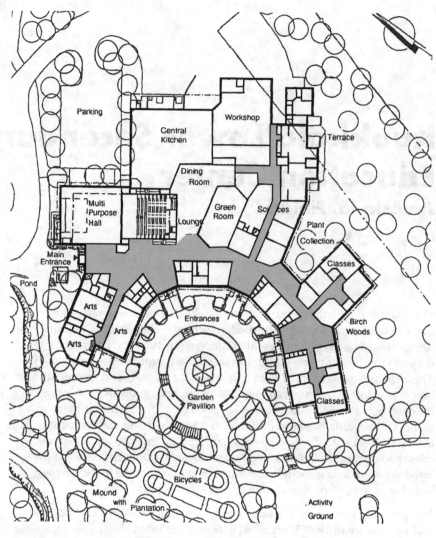

Site Plan
The school is set in a park-like setting that is designed as an ecological learning environment.

Below: The school dining room looks onto the Green Room

Eco-Park

The design of the school seeks to combine concern for the protection of the natural environment and increased use of technology. The theme "man, nature and building" is emphasized in the pedagogical approach and the architectural design for the school. The curving internal street and location of glazing within the building are designed to open the interior of the building to the surrounding natural wooded landscape of birches and pine trees. In this way, it is intended that students and teachers will gain an appreciation for the natural environment and develop a long term interest in protecting it.

The building design features several environmental learning spaces and special features to aid the ecology-based curriculum. The Green Room is a glass enclosed "green house" that extends between the suite of science classrooms and the dining room, for use by both areas. The Green Room will house a wide variety of plants to be used in teaching and research. Natural Finnish stones are used in the floor and the walls for both aesthetic and educational purposes. It is also designed to bring daylight and vegetation into the center of the building, enlivening the dining room and the interior street.

The Garden Pavilion is a gathering place for students and teachers to the southwest of the school building. It is nestled in the curve of the school on one side and landscaped grounds on the other. The grounds are designed as an ecological laboratory including gardens, woods and a compost area.

BUILDING DESIGN

The building is organized with an internal "street" which is intended to be the "communicating" link through the school. The street is not only for circulation (as is the traditional school corridor), but also to meet, to talk and even to work.

The internal street is curved in plan, with learning areas arranged in "neighborhoods" along its path. The school's principal likens the space to the main street of a small town, with interesting things to look at (i.e., student work) and opportunities for people to meet. From this perspective, the curve in the street has an important design intention: to create an intimate scale that promotes interaction and cooperation amongst students and teachers. To support this purpose, five student lounges are located along the street for group and project work. Classroom suites, other shared learning spaces, and the dining room are arranged along this corridor, all considered part of the "town."

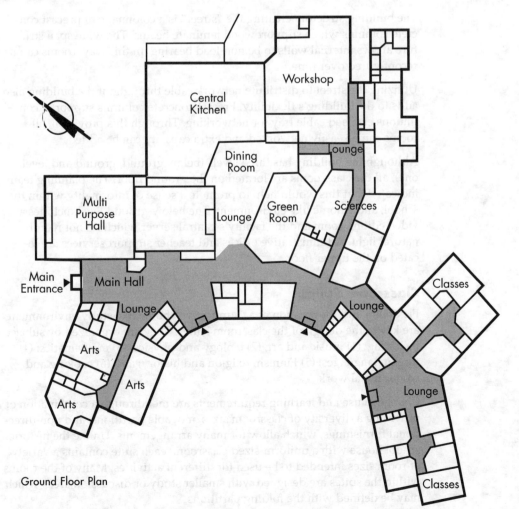

Ground Floor Plan

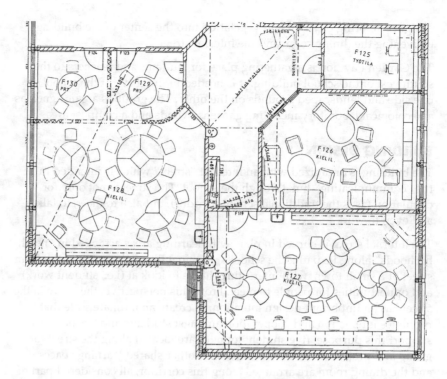

Plan Detail
Classroom suites are designed as "home like" spaces with rooms of various size allowing students and teachers to choose the space most suited to their work.

The building structure creating the "street" is a colonnade of precast concrete columns which support wood laminate beams. The wide span structure allows internal walls to be non-load bearing. In this way, rooms can be reconfigured over time.

Utilizing the street to distribute network cable throughout the building also adds to the building's flexibility. Precast concrete columns support a continuous exposed cable tray for networking. Through this provision, all rooms can be easily networked and extra capacity can be added.

Although the building has three levels (below ground, ground and level one), all the classrooms are located on the ground floor. The planning team indicated that this would help to promote a sense of informality within the school, and a home like environment. The below-ground level includes a video editing room and the facility's central server which do not require natural light. Administrative offices and teacher support services are located on the upper floor.

Classroom Suites

Flexibility and the creation of a "supportive" home like study environment are key to the design of the classroom suites. They are organized by subject including: (1) music and art; (2) biology and physics; (3) mathematics; (4) foreign languages; (5) Finnish, religion and history; and (6) cooking and wood/metal work.

Change in use and learning requirements are met through a combination of providing a diversity of classroom sizes, movable partitions, and non-directional furnishings, which allow for many arrangements. Unlike the historic school house with a uniform-sized classroom, each suite contains a variety of room sizes intended to be used for different activities. Many of the rooms within the suites are designed with smaller study or discussion areas which may be defined with the folding partitions.

To allow the rooms to be rearranged easily, several types of "non-directional" desks (see classroom plan) have been designed for these classrooms. The integrated colors of the furnishings will support the overall flexibility. Many of the rooms have been designed without a teacher's desk. Instead, teachers are given work space or office space on the second floor of the building. In this way, the teacher is not associated with a specific room. At the same time, the absence of the teacher's desk is intended to imply a change in the role of the teacher within the classroom.

INFORMATION TECHNOLOGY

Rather than specifying technology at the outset, the planning team chose two strategies: (1) to select the technology at the end of the building phase to assure the most current equipment available; and (2) to develop a flexible network distribution that will accommodate technology changes that will be made during the life of the building.

The building is networked with a local area network to file servers. Students may contact data bases, use electronic mail and make other connections via the network. Video meetings for distance learning and discussion with other schools are also possible.

Each classroom will include at least one computer with additional technology to be introduced according to need. Ultimately, the planners envision all students having their own portable computer. They believe that the use of portable computers will best meet the school's educational goals and help create a "small town" which allows for "open" learning. Two special rooms will include a concentration of computers for student use. A video editing center is provided because multimedia is seen as becoming an important aspect of students' work.

RESEARCH AND EVALUATION

The planning and development of this school is the subject of study by faculty from the Institute for Educational Research at the University of Jyväskylä who have had an important role in the school's development. The research focuses on three aspects of the school's development: planning, construction and effectiveness. A follow-up study is planned to collect data through questionnaires and interviews with persons involved in the planning and construction of the schools. Students, teachers and other users will also be interviewed after the school has opened.

KEY POINTS

- The school provides a learning environment that seeks to unite respect for the natural environment and information technology.

- It uses an internal street as an organizing principle, to provide networking throughout the building, and to promote communication amongst students and teachers.

- The building has been designed to be flexible and accommodate future change through easily reconfigurable internal space.

REFERENCES

Rask, Sauli. "The Kuokkala School Project." AERA Annual Meeting, April 20-24, 1993: 1-24.

Above: A double height interior "street" is the main organizing feature for the building plan.

Above right: Exterior view of the entrance to Thomas Telford School.

Right: Students working in one of three class areas within a learning base.

Thomas Telford School

Telford, England

The Thomas Telford School, completed in 1992, is one of 15 schools built or renovated under the United Kingdom's City Technology College (CTC) initiative. Through this initiative the planning team for the Telford school sought to "implement an innovative curriculum with a particular emphasis on technology and science, aided by the widespread use of information technology."

New construction
Occupied: 1991-1992
14-18 months to develop
Cost: £10.8 million equipped
Potential enrollment:
1000 students

Architects: Barnsley, Hewett & Mallinson

City Technology Colleges

In 1986, the CTC initiative was funded by a collaboration of government, private business and industry. The CTCs were to address two main goals: to emphasize science and technology curriculum and to develop new school management practices. "Technology studies" are one of 10 subject areas covered in the UK's national curriculum. The CTCs are distinctive in that no less than 30 percent (but not more than 40 percent) of academic study is devoted to technology and science.

The City Technology Colleges were to be located in inner city areas. There is no fee associated with enrollment. The school buildings are either new construction or renovations of existing facilities. The resulting City Technology Colleges are attractive, innovative and interesting.

Thomas Telford School

The building design for the Thomas Telford School addressed three goals: (1) to provide access to information technology and networked data bases throughout the school, enhanced by the use of "resource centers"; (2) to create an environment which would allow for both class-based instruction, and independent learning to take place; and (3) to create a flexible learning environment which will allow for team teaching, expanded enrollment and change over time.

The technology distribution strategy combines individualized student use of portable computers, distribution of networked computer workstations throughout the school, and a school-wide network to help support these design goals. All students are loaned a personal portable computer (or laptop) for use throughout their enrollment. As many educators look toward the portable computer being standard equipment for education in the future, the design solutions for this building should be of particular interest.

The school was built for a capacity of 1,000 students. At the time of this research (1993), 700 students were enrolled. The headmaster projected that total enrollment could rise to 1,300 students by 1994-95 due to interest in the program and through strategies to extend the use of the facility while reducing capital costs through distance learning.

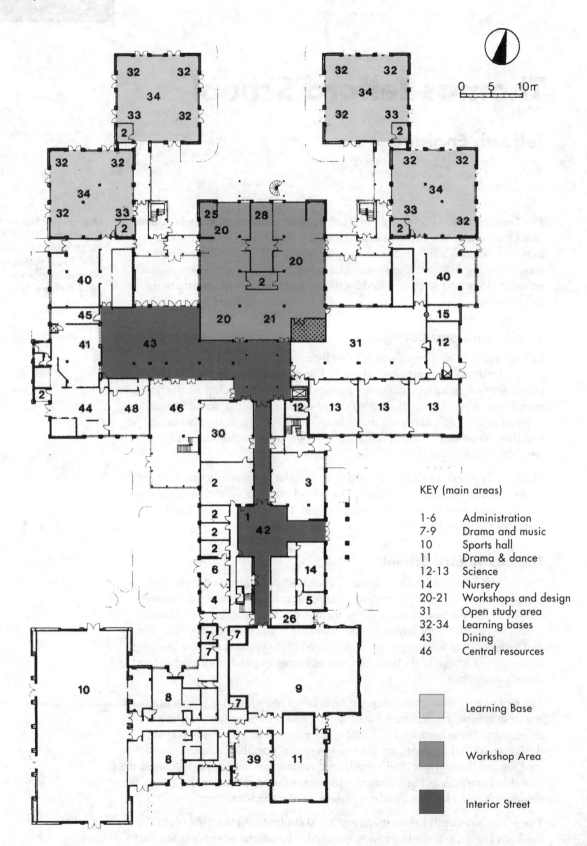

KEY (main areas)

1-6	Administration
7-9	Drama and music
10	Sports hall
11	Drama & dance
12-13	Science
14	Nursery
20-21	Workshops and design
31	Open study area
32-34	Learning bases
43	Dining
46	Central resources

Learning Base

Workshop Area

Interior Street

Ground Floor Plan

CURRICULUM

An educational team, which included the future principal of the school, developed the school's curriculum to incorporate the National Curriculum. The National Curriculum specifies the use of Information Technology (IT) across the curriculum, as well as a specific component to teach IT awareness, skills, and processes as an adjunct to the design and technology curriculum.

Teachers in each of the school's six "areas of experience" are responsible for curriculum development. Fifty percent of the teachers' time is devoted to teaching, using equal time for curriculum development, preparation, administration, and counseling. Teacher training is an important component of the program, and is conducted both in-house and externally.

Due to the demands of the curriculum, the school week is 25 percent longer than average (starting earlier and ending later). Students attend school 40 weeks of the year. "Homework Center" allows students to study in the building until as late as 8:30 p.m. As well, parental "ownership" or investment in the school is viewed as one key to the success of the program.

Information technology resource areas exist throughout the school. Pictured above is a resource area located within a "Learning Base."

BUILDING DESIGN

The architects were asked to articulate their interpretation of the curriculum in the building design. In addition, they were required to develop technical solutions to potential difficulties in satisfying the inclusion of information technology in teaching and management. The resulting design reflected the administrators' request that the building "reflect working environments in the 21st century." The design for Thomas Telford School had three aims:

- To apply new technologies comprehensively, providing access to IT equipment throughout the school as well as in specialized "resource centers";
- To allow for a diversity of teaching and learning spaces which would facilitate instruction in class groups and independent study by students; and
- To provide flexibility to accommodate increases in student enrollment and changes of use over time.

The building is organized around an interior, double height "street" which is the main access corridor leading to workshops, subject-based instructional areas, such as business education and science, and the "learning bases" or class suites. The workshop areas are for design, manufacture, arts, and materials. The workshops have an open plan and are visible from the main corridor through glazed partitions. A zone for computer workstations is included within the workshops for use by students and teachers.

Inclusion of a reception area inside the school's entrance was intended as a statement of the school's openness to the community. Choices of interior colors and architectural details further add to the welcoming impression. Rather than checking in at their learning base at the beginning of the day, the students register for the day electronically using a personal swipe card at an electronic reader.

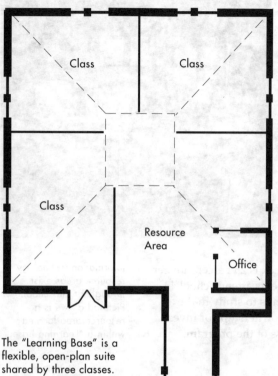

The "Learning Base" is a flexible, open-plan suite shared by three classes. The suite includes a shared technology "resource area" and an enclosed teachers' office.

Learning Base: Flexible Learning Suite

The "Learning Base" is an independent suite which houses three classes. Each suite includes a shared technology area, designated as the resource center, and an office. The suite features an open plan under a hipped roof. The sky-lit roof is supported by laminated beams and steel bracing creating a column-free space. This allows for flexible use and reconfiguration of the suite's space with low movable partitions. These partitions are generally organized to divide the suite into three classrooms and a resource area. Movable student lockers are provided within the suite and also help to divide the space. Carpeting is provided for acoustic attenuation.

The teachers' work area is a glazed office looking onto the resource center in each suite. This work area allows for teacher preparation, curriculum development, and promotes exchange between the teachers within a suite.

Based upon the initial years of use, the administrators indicated that the suite concept could have been extended throughout the school. The open plan has been far more successful than expected, providing an environment in which teachers work together with ease.

TECHNOLOGY

The school's planners developed a strategy to provide access to information technology as a resource on several levels: to the individual; to the class; to a cluster of classes; to subject areas, as well as school-wide; to the home; and, by 1996, community-wide. Four elements address this strategy: (1) creation of a building-wide network with the library as its hub; (2) assignment of personal portable computers to each student for home and school use; (3) networked computer workstations distributed throughout the school; and (4) use of all available means of communication including modem, "cable" and satellite to access and deliver information beyond the school.

Network

The school's network hub is located in the library which functions as the central information and resource center. The school is networked for CD-ROM, data and video, utilizing 11 file servers. Access to external data via the Internet and Campus 2000 is also possible. A microwave receiver allows for receipt of diverse educational programming. Two satellite dishes provide access to satellite broadcasts such as weather data and foreign language programs. Students and teachers access resources from open study and resource areas throughout the school. As a result, the required size of the library has been minimized.

Portables

All students are assigned a portable computer to use during their enrollment in the school The use of the portable is intended to extend the technology-based learning experience to the home, and to allow flexibility within the school. The school originally selected relatively low-cost portables and complemented these low-power machines with networked computer workstations within the classroom suites. In this way, files from the portables could be downloaded onto a workstation for further work.

Networked computer workstations are located throughout the school. A minimum of 12 are provided per Learning Base. One or two workstations are located in each class area, and the remainder are located within each base's resource center for use by students and teachers. The bases have raised floors (double floors) to allow for ease of networking and access to power. Desks and other furnishings include cable management trays to distribute electric service and networking cables to each work area.

Distance Learning: Community and Home Access

The school also plans to provide a distance learning center. Distance learning is predicted to alter the school's approach to educational delivery in a number of ways. In addition to providing more educational services to the community, the administrators envision the potential to expand enrollment without additional capital expenditure for new building construction. With a combination of double sessions and at-home learning via multimedia-style distance communication, a doubling of the enrollment capacity is seen as being possible. By 1996, the administrators predict students will complete at least 20 percent of their learning activities at home via distance communication.

Each "Learning Base" has a canopy-like roof which allows for an open floor plan and structure-free space. The skylight brings light into the center of the suite. The exposed wood and metal roof structure adds warmth and architectural interest to the suite.

KEY POINTS

- School provides access to information technology for students and the community.

- Design features innovative, open-plan learning bases which allow for flexibility and team teaching.

- All students are provided with portable computers for school and home use.

- School plans to use distance learning to extend the enrollment of the school and to make educational resources available to the community.

REFERENCES

Thompson, Andy, et al. *Educational Design Initiatives in City Technology Colleges: Building Bulletin 72.* London: The Department of Education and Science, 1991. See "Thomas Telford School" supplement.

Left and below: All students at MLC use portable computers in their studies.

A key aspect of the changes taking place at MLC is the change of focus from instruction of students by the teacher, to learning by doing, where the student constructs her own learning, with the help of the teacher.

Jeff Burn, Di Fleming and Margaret Fallshaw
Methodist Ladies' College

Methodist Ladies' College

Kew, Victoria, Australia

"Students become teachers (as well as learners) and teachers become learners (as well as teachers)."

David Loader, Principal, MLC

This example presents a school building designed specifically for the use of portable computers, which many educators anticipate will become standard equipment for all students. Methodist Ladies' College (MLC) is an independent college for female students ages six to 18. The school's administrators and faculty have recently sought to re-frame the educational experience from being "teacher-centered" to being "student-centered." The college intends that the curriculum will be less fixed, with students more able, in the words of Seymour Papert, "to construct their own learning." Teachers are viewed as facilitators as well as fellow learners. The Harold Wood Wing is located in a renovated building on the MLC campus. The renovation reflects the needs of this new kind of learning environment, by providing space to work independently from the teacher, whether individually or in groups.

The setting emphasizes personal rather than school computing (there are no computer labs). An important tool to achieve this goal was the introduction of portable computers. Educators at MLC believe this tool has the potential to change the way knowledge is acquired and to influence rethinking the educational environment. As a result of the use of information technology, the MLC faculty envision a learning environment which is not tied to a specific location, what the principal refers to a "dispersed campus" concept.

Changing the Context for Learning

Rather than developing computer labs or computer-equipped classrooms, MLC decided in 1990 to require students to buy or lease their own portable computers. The principal asked the teachers at all grade levels to adopt the concept. Grade five teachers agreed to include the use of portables in the curriculum and to require that all students entering the grade have a personal computer. Since that time, the success and popularity of their use has resulted in all teachers from grades five to 10 agreeing to work with portables. Approximately 70 percent of the students in grades 11 and 12 have also leased or purchased portables voluntarily. The leasing option is popular with more than 50 percent choosing it. Advantages of the personal computer include the application of a personal work station beyond the classroom to the library or science lab, and to be able to use it while on excursions or in the college's remote educational site located 500 kilometers from MLC at the perimeter of a wilderness zone.

Renovation
Occupied: Fall 1993
Architect: Daryl Jackson Pty. Ltd.
Total number of students: 2200
Junior School, year 5 – 6
Junior Secondary School,
year 7 – 8
Middle School, year 9 – 10
Senior School, year 11 – 12

Many of the benefits of the personal computer were just what we had hoped for when we began the program, but the exciting thing was the synergistic effects that were over and above what we had envisaged. Technology proved to be more than a catalyst for change in learning and teaching practises; it also ushered in an entirely new culture in which the school became a community of learners, where co-operative and collaborative learning became the norm.

Irene Grasso, Assistant to the Principal, MLC

Architects working with teachers and administrators, developed a "Learning Unit Model" to facilitate the ubiquitous use of laptop computers, and associated change in learning methods. The components of this unit include flexible learning areas, staff area, resource area, and rooms for meetings and independent work by students. These spaces are connected visually with use of glazing and by the organization of the plan. The goal of the design is to support a high level of interaction between students and teachers.

The Teacher's Role

The introduction of laptops has meant that staff need to be supported in ways that enable them to cope with their changing professional environment. . . . The view is taken by MLC that the school needs to be redesigned to make it into a learning place for teachers as well as students.

David Loader, Principal

Adopting the use of portables, and a more "student-centered" approach to education placed special demands on the teachers. At the same time, they needed to become proficient in the use of the technology and amenable to the changes that come with it. Teachers are viewed as facilitators of a student's pursuit of knowledge and skills. To this end, more time has been allocated for professional and curriculum development.

These changes at MLC now allow learning to occur in many ways. Some instruction occurs according to a seminar, or conference, model. Lectures are given to large groups; students then meet in smaller discussion or task-oriented groups. Interdisciplinary study is encouraged as students learn to develop inquiry-based investigations.

BUILDING DESIGN

The Harold Wood Wing renovation created an open learning suite on each of the building's three floors. Each suite comprises the elements of the "learning model unit" with rooms similar to "traditional" classrooms, a resource area, a staff room, a locker room and other support spaces. The open learning suite concept hinges on two ideas: that there should be a physical, visual, and electronic connection between the spaces; and that the resource area should form a hub at the center of the various learning spaces. In this way, the goal of the "learning model unit" was to create a system of spaces, rather than discreet classrooms.

The resource area is used for group instruction and for collaborative work. Overall, it is viewed as a place for students to work on projects independently or with students from other classes. The intention of the resource area was to provide a minimum of furniture, to allow for flexible use. Students work on the carpeted floor, which was observed as the preferred location for student group work. Three risers (steps) run the full length of one wall for an amphitheater effect. Printers and other peripheral technology are located in the area. Construction, modeling, experimentation, robotics and other activities take place within a tiled area with a sink. Double doors and generous amounts of glazing between the other spaces and the resource

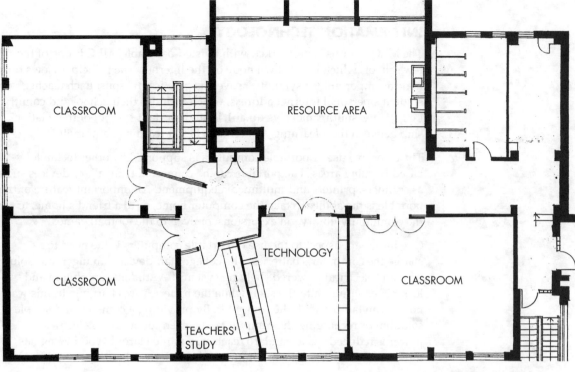

Each learning suite
groups three classrooms
around a core area
comprised of the resource
area, the technology room
and the teachers' study.

area allow for physical and visual connection. The smaller spaces are appropriate for small group presentations, discussion groups and task orientation activities.

Additional learning spaces are located in specific suites. A library for the three suites is located on the ground level and the *Lego Logo* robotics resource room is found on the second floor.

A teachers' room is included in each suite to encourage a team approach to teaching and in professional development. Teachers can assist each other exploring new teaching methods. Again, like the student, the teacher becomes a "learner" in the technology-based learning environment. The teachers' room is physically and visually connected to the rest of the suite.

Students work together
informally in the resource
area.

Diagram: Conceptual organization of the learning suite.

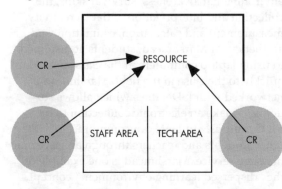

INFORMATION TECHNOLOGY

The MLC campus is networked with twisted pair cable. MLC is one of the few schools which has its own node on the Internet. The principal views this node as important for symbolic as well as practical reasons. Each teacher's or student's personal Internet address, which includes their school and country (e.g. Jenny_smith@mlckew.edu.au), is an important symbol of the relationship between their learning "space" to a larger learning community.

The extensive use of portable computers is supported by other technology-based learning areas. The portable can be connected to ancillary devices such as scanners, printers and multimedia equipment. An important feature of the portable is the ability to take the computer home, or to a friend's home, to the community library, on excursions, or even to the football game.

One important aspect to the use of portable computers is the need to re-charge the computer's batteries. The college staff devised an ingenious solution: an "electrical powered shelving system." A student can plug in and lock her computer into the shelf while the batteries are charging. In this way no one can tamper with the computer. By providing a compact and simple solution for recharging the computers, the need for access to electrical power is reduced. As a standard, each area in the Harold Wood Wing has three network ports and a minimum of three electrical outlets.

Marshmead

The paradigm chosen for Marshmead was a comfortable home in a village and not a tent in the bush . . . there are daily chores . . . (and) citizenship responsibilities relating to the maintenance of the community.

David Loader
"As I Would Like It"

Students at Marshmead readily adapt to using their portables in the field.

MLC's remote Marshmead campus is located 500 kilometers from the main campus in a temperate rain forest at the edge of a designated wilderness area. The educational program at Marshmead combines an investigation of the natural world with technology-based learning. In year nine (age 14-15), all MLC students spend eight weeks at Marshmead, exploring a part of the Australian wilderness and learning about the environment.

The curriculum focuses on effective communication and decision making skills, community and environmental awareness, survival skills, the collection and interpretation of data, creativity, measurement and calculation, estimation, and aesthetics. At Marshmead, students accustomed to using laptop computers in the classroom adapt quickly to their use in the field. Marshmead is networked with ISDN lines which allows students to make an electronic connection to the MLC campus. Students can communicate with other students and teachers through an electronic message service. Marshmead is one example of the "dispersed learning environment" concept.

DISPERSED CAMPUS CONCEPT

Educators at Methodist Ladies' College view the classroom as a useful model of the past which is no longer applicable to today's education. In replacement, they envision dispersed and flexible settings for learning. The overarching goal is to give students independence, authority, opportunity and access. The school as a place for learning remains important, but the emphasis of its use should be on exchange between students and teachers, and between students and students for collaborative work and for community experiences. The home can become a better extension of the school with the use of the portable workstation. Another possible outcome of this change is the reallocation of resources to support greater use of technology and staff development.

The Harold Wood Wing renovation is a first step in exploring how the physical setting should respond to the use of portable computers. Initially, there was a need to test the idea of using portable computers and demonstrate success before full implementation was possible. Similarly, the design of the open learning unit could have been taken further, according to the principal. However, with time, the concept of the "dispersed campus" may meet with greater acceptance and yield more interesting physical models.

As the Harold Wood Wing was being designed and constructed, MLC developed a much larger project with the architect Daryl Jackson, a music school. The same concepts were applied to the music school incorporating the portable computer as a mobile workstation into the learning environment. The music school will provide for people meeting "in performance," formally and informally. The exchange of ideas in the process of changing the learning unit points toward a new description of a place for learning. The context of this place for learning is the portable workstation and exchange between students.

KEY POINTS

- The college uses laptop computers to support student-centered learning.

- Professional development, planning and curriculum development are considered essential activities for the faculty.

- Student-centered learning is supported by open learning suites composed of flexible learning areas, staff accommodation, resource areas, individual work and meeting rooms.

- The use of portable computers and other technologies supports dispersed learning, as seen at MLC Marshmead, the college's remote location.

REFERENCES

Daryl Jackson Pty. Ltd., Architects. *Methodist Ladies' College: 1992 Masterplan*. "Executive Summary." Section 1.6.

Grasso, Irene and Margaret Fallshaw, eds. *Reflections Of A Learning Community*. Victoria, Australia: Methodist Ladies' College, March 1993.

Shipp, Heather. "The Marshmead Curriculum." *The Star*. [Quarterly magazine published for the MLC community.] Vol. 6, No. 4. 1992, p.8.

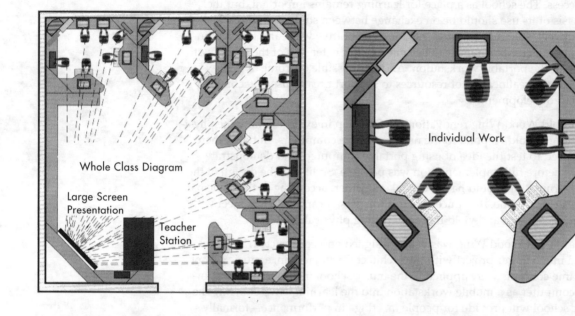

Whole Class Diagram

Large Screen
Presentation

Teacher
Station

Individual Work

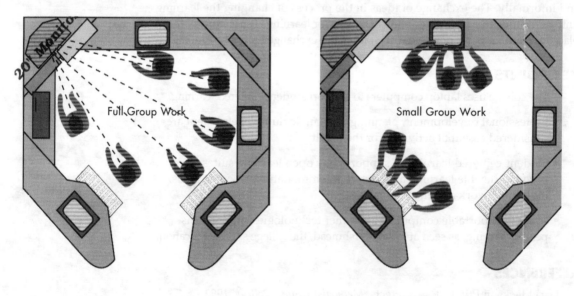

20" Monitor

Full Group Work

Small Group Work

Blackstock Junior High School

Port Hueneme, California, USA

Blackstock Junior High School is the centerpiece of the Hueneme School District's efforts, under the leadership of Superintendent Ronald Rescigno, to integrate the use of information technology into the schools and the curriculum. Beginning in the mid-1980s, a group of teachers and administrators developed the concept of the "Smart Classroom." Architect Scott Ellinwood was hired to bring the concept into reality, and the first of eleven prototype classroom designs resulted.

Blackstock Junior High School has since installed specially outfitted classrooms for Math, Science, Social Studies, English as a Second Language (ESL) and Language Arts. The library is also designated as a "smart" area. The remaining classrooms in the school are fully networked with access to the Internet as well as a district-wide educational network. Each classroom in the school contains at least ten computers.

Through the district LAN classes taught at Blackstock are transmitted to other locations in the district where students can view the instruction on television monitors. In addition, the administrative offices are fully networked utilizing information technology for purposes of record keeping and assessment.

Renovation
Junior HighSchool
Size:807 students
Architect:
Scott Ellinwood & Associates
Ventura, California

Building Design

Blackstock Junior High School was built in the early 1960s. The classrooms are standard 30 X 30 foot rooms arranged around an open central courtyard. Several smaller light courts are introduced at various locations to provide natural light to each room. The administrative and common areas are grouped along one side of the courtyard.

The school is organized into three academic "houses": Humanities, Human Resources and Technology. The Humanities house is associated with two "smart" classrooms for social studies and language arts, and the library. Under "Human Resources" are grouped Music, Fine Arts, Physical Education and the "Career Center". The third house, Technology, is associated with a science lab, a math lab and a technology lab.

Interactive Learning Environments

The Hueneme School District uses the term "Smart Classroom" to designate a classroom dedicated for the use of information technology in education. The "smart" classroom is outfitted with multimedia computer and presentation equipment and is fully networked. The physical layout of each room has been developed specifically for the educational activities that take place in the room.

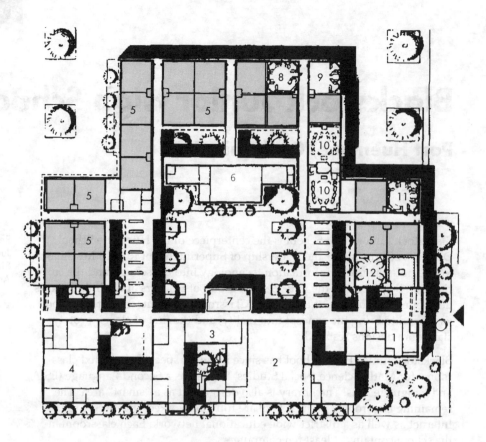

LEGEND

1 adminstration
2 cafeteria
3 teachers lounge
4 Smart Lab
5 classrooms
6 library
7 stage
8 Smart Language
9 Smart ESL
10 Smart Science
11 Smart Social Studies
12 Smart Math

Computer monitors are placed below the desk top to provide a flat, uncluttered work surface.

First prototype

The first prototype "smart" classroom was installed in the mid-1980s, a time when the problems of integrating computers into the classroom were still quite new and unexplored. The architect designed special furniture for the classroom to accommodate the computer equipment and cabling. The classroom is organized into five clusters of six students arranged around the perimeter of the room. Each cluster incorporates appropriate voice, video, data networking and multimedia technology: monitors (free standing and built-in), keyboards, hard drives and other peripherals such as VCR's, external drives, scanners and CD ROM. The network enables the teacher to send information to a student as well as observe students as they work.

One of the design innovations implemented was placing the computer monitors, as well as the CPU and peripheral equipment, below the work surface. Students view the monitor through a pane of glass set into the desk surface. The keyboard is held in a drawer which slides out for use.

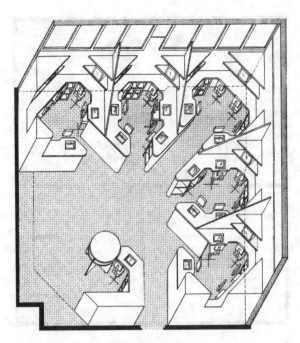

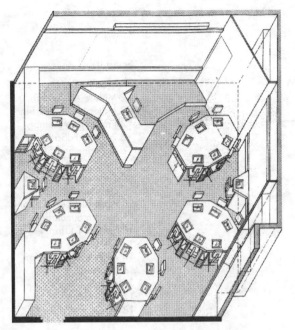

Left: The first protoype "Smart" classroom.
Above: The eleventh prototype "Smart" Math classroom.

This allows for a large uncluttered work surface and eliminates any visual barrier between the students and the teacher. Each cluster also includes a large screen monitor for use during group work. All cabling is kept out of sight and out of the way. In this way, the technology does not receive undue attention by the simple virtue of its visibility. The technology is completely functional as an educational tool without the usual distracting clutter.

"Smart" Math Classroom

The "smart" Math classroom represents the eleventh prototype classroom in the Hueneme School District. In this model, students workstations are clustered in groups of six at five large work tables called "turtles". Students face each other to facilitate interaction and cooperative learning. As with the previous models, all equipment, including monitors is located beneath the desk top to provide a flat, uncluttered work surface. Cabling is concealed but accessible and storage for such devices as mice, earphones and microphones is provided for in a compartment in the center of the table.

Teacher's workstation.

The teacher's workstation sits on a raised platform. The teacher's equipment includes a monitor, CPU, color printer and color scanner all beneath the desk top. A ceiling-mounted overhead projector and motorized screen are controlled from the teacher's work station. A 35 inch television is also located in the classroom. Behind the teacher an infrared electronic blackboard, connected to the file server, is mounted on the wall. Located in a closet are the network hub and connections, the classroom file server and a seven-bay CD ROM tower. The lighting is designed to eliminate glare on the glass panels in the desk tops.

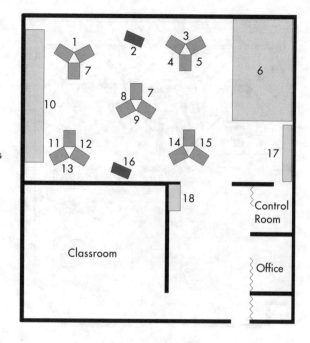

Smart Lab

 1 Product Development
 2 Mobile AV Station
 3 Materials Processing
 4 Prototype Assembly
 5 Product Fabrication
 6 Experimental Structures
 7 CAD/CAM
 8 Telecommunications
 9 Desktop Publishing
10 Performance Test Zone
11 System Simulation
12 Vehicle Design
13 AIR LINK
14 Architectural Design
15 Structural Systems
16 Mobile Storage
17 Hydroponics
18 Research Station

The classroom is also equipped with two video cameras for broadcast. One camera focuses on the students and the other on the teacher. The cameras are activated by microphones at the student work tables and a wireless microphone which the teacher wears.

Smart Lab

Blackstock Junior High School also developed a technology laboratory in conjunction with a private company, Transtech Systems. The prototype lab was developed at Blackstock and the vendor now markets the system as a "turnkey" technology lab. A small gymnasium was renovated for the Smart Lab providing an open and flexible space. The "Smart Lab" is an integrated system of furnishings, equipment, computer-mediated instruction, software and in-service training. Technology is used as a tool to strengthen critical thinking, conceptualization, discovery, problem solving, and decision-making skills.

Work islands in the "Smart Lab" consist of three work stations radiating from a center power and services conduit.

The lab is organized as a series of work islands. The islands are designed for sequential learning activities. As students move from station to station, they can choose to work in teams or individually. Each station has a different function and operates independently from the others. Student activities integrate all phases of design, manufacturing, production and marketing.

Each work island consists of three work/learn stations radiating from a service column for provision of electricity, compressed air and network cabling. Each island is mobile to allow reconfiguration of the setting. Key features of this system include:

• Modular elements and furnishings,

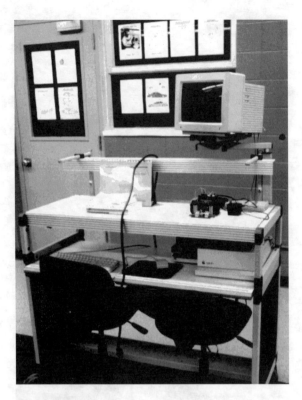

Mobile workstation in the "Smart Lab".

- Inter-connectable workstations,
- Reconfigurable workstations and
- Cost-effectiveness

The "Smart Lab" provides a technology education course that allows students to get hands-on experience in a variety of areas. It is an educational setting that encourages active learning and interaction among students.

Conclusion

Blackstock Junior High School has been in the forefront developing approaches to integrating computers and technology into the curriculum. The renovation of existing classrooms over the course of a decade, has allowed them to transform and refine their model classroom of the future.

Key Points

- Specially designed and outfitted technology-rich classrooms for instruction in Math Science, Languages, English and Social Studies,

- Comprehensive technology instruction lab,

- Business–education partnerships,

- All classrooms networked and have at least ten computers,

- District-wide educational network, and

- Renovation of existing school building.

References

Rescigno, Ronald C., Ed.D., "Prototype 11th Generation Hueneme School District Smart Classroom: Math", Port Hueneme, California:Hueneme School District, May 1994.

Above: The internal street serves as public place where students and teachers meet.

Above right: The entrance to New Leith Academy shows the outline of the internal street.

Right: Power and network cabling are supplied to desktops via a ceiling grid and power poles.

New Leith Academy

Edinburgh, Scotland

The design of this "school of the future" features four key elements: (1) a modular system provides flexibility for change; (2) an internal "street" facilitates community access, ease of circulation, and energy efficiency; (3) provision for the increasing use of information technology is included; and (4) references to vernacular architecture humanize the scale of the building.

The designers sought to develop a school that would meet current educational requirements and also be adaptable in the future. They projected that the life span of a school building is more than 60 years. During this time, the building's users and their needs may change. Therefore, the design should allow for modifications in the plan and use of the school.

The building has been primarily designed as a place for learning for students and adults, though it also allows for concurrent use as a community and recreation center. In responding to current trends in education and to the demands placed on a school by a variety of different users, the designers took into consideration increasing demand for adult education, particularly to train and retrain workers for an increasingly technological society.

The designers' approach was to create a welcoming and flexible building that could be adapted to a variety of learning situations without major renovations. In addition, the strategy was designed to address problems of growth or decline. If, for example, the size of the student population declines, some areas of the building can be adapted for office or commercial use.

BUILDING DESIGN

New Leith Academy is a newly constructed secondary school, replacing an existing one in the port district of Edinburgh. It is located on the site of a former factory, adjacent to a residential neighborhood to the west and an industrial area to the east. In response, the residential side of the school is a single story, and the two-story portions of the school are located on the eastern, industrial side. The school has an enrollment of 900 students, but it is designed for community use and can accommodate 1,500 people at one time.

New construction
Occupied: 1991
Architect: Laura Stevenson
Number of students: 900

Clerestory windows create more useable space at the perimeter of the classroom.

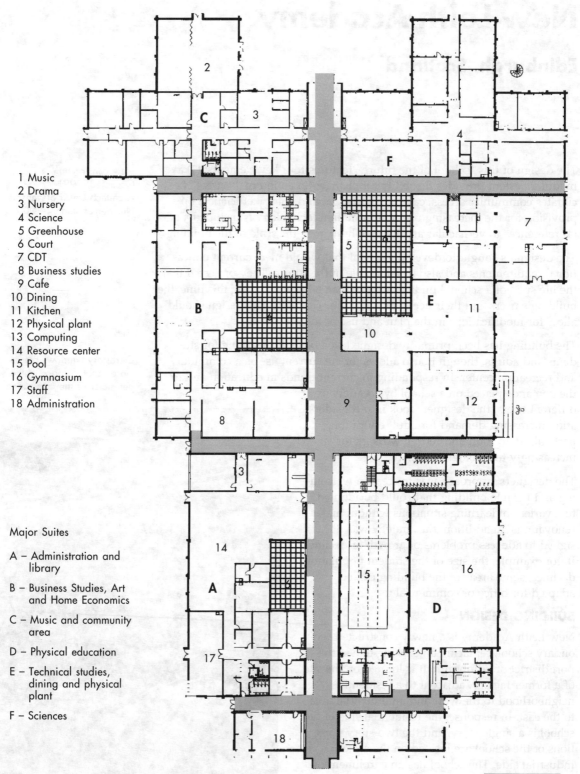

1 Music
2 Drama
3 Nursery
4 Science
5 Greenhouse
6 Court
7 CDT
8 Business studies
9 Cafe
10 Dining
11 Kitchen
12 Physical plant
13 Computing
14 Resource center
15 Pool
16 Gymnasium
17 Staff
18 Administration

Major Suites

A – Administration and library

B – Business Studies, Art and Home Economics

C – Music and community area

D – Physical education

E – Technical studies, dining and physical plant

F – Sciences

0 2.4 6.0 9.6   16.8   24.0m

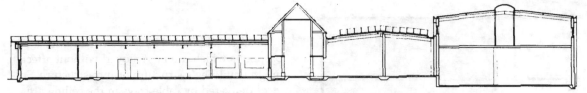

New Leith Academy uses a modular dimensioning system to create a rational and flexible design. This approach is utilized at every scale of design: the building, the individual room, furniture design, and architectural details. The building is designed to allow for increases and decreases in student enrollment. The strategy allows for growth in enrollment of up to 40 percent, or for radical contraction and reuse of the facility.

The modular dimensioning system allows the building to be developed incrementally. The system is based on a 16.8 meter module consisting of three bays: one 2.4 m wide bay set between two 7.2 m wide bays. The center bay is skylit, bringing daylight deep into the building and may or may not be used for circulation. The dimensioning system also regulates the placement of the cable trays, lighting and other services in the grid which allows flexibility to make alterations within the school.

Access to information technology is provided throughout New Leith Academy; the cabling infrastructure is not limited to certain areas or activities. Trunking is installed in all corridors providing connections to electricity, electronic data, and telecommunications throughout the building. Within classrooms and seminar rooms, ceiling-hung cable trays, power poles and wall-mounted trunking provide connections to power and networking.

In an effort to create a human-scale environment that is "student-friendly", the architects employed ideas expressed by Christopher Alexander in *A Pattern Language* in which he documents vernacular architecture as a reference for architectural design. Modular variations in the dimension of the street generate features such as small seating areas and planters creating a welcoming environment.

Internal Street

A glazed main "street" provides the organizing feature of the building. This street is the major axis of the building and serves as the primary circulation route. Academic departments and social spaces, including administrative offices, the library, the cafe, and the school's three courtyards, are directly accessible from this street. In addition, building's systems including local cooling units, air handling units, and power are routed through the street. The glazing allows for the capture of solar heat as well as the containment of internally produced heat for energy savings in colder weather.

Pedestrian circulation and distribution of services are further provided by secondary and tertiary pathways. The main street is bisected by three cross streets that organize the building into six sub-blocks, or suites. This secondary circulation permits the various parts of the building to function independently, thus allowing the building to serve multiple users. Tertiary paths provide circulation within the suites.

Top: East–West section shows the organization of the building: the single-story portion of the school to the east, the double-height internal street in the center and the two-story portion to the west.

Below: An axonometric drawing shows the internal street and the provision for delivery of power, networking and environmental systems through that space.

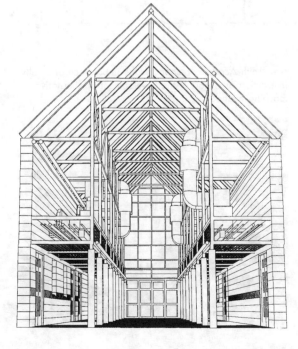

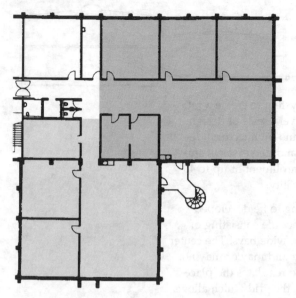

Classroom suites, (above) designed according to the modular dimensioning system, (below) provide spaces for a variety of educational uses.

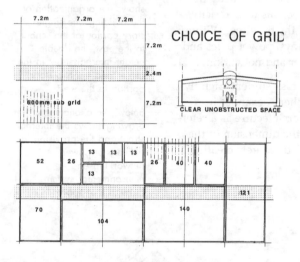

New Leith Academy recognizes the importance of faculty interaction as a part of the development of alternative teaching methods.

Each suite is bounded by non-structural masonry partitions which can be removed without affecting the building's structure or infrastructure. Services delivered by cable trays in the ceiling are easily reconfigured when partitions are moved.

Classroom Organization

Classrooms, laboratories and other learning spaces are organized according to suites, providing a variety of learning environments. All suites consist of classrooms, seminar spaces, shared study spaces and rooms for the teaching staff. The school's dimensioning system allows for a variety of classroom sizes within each suite suitable for different learning situations: class meeting space, seminar spaces for small group discussions and cooperative work, shared study space, independent study areas and social space. Laboratories include computer rooms adjacent to the library, an information technology-based business lab and the science labs.

Teachers' Area

New Leith Academy emphasizes the role of the teacher as a facilitator for learning. The administration recognizes the need for in-service training for teachers to learn new teaching methods and to help put them into practice. In addition, teachers require space for preparation as well as for cooperative work with their colleagues in exploring new ideas, materials and techniques. All learning suites include space dedicated for teacher use. In addition, a generous staff room and several seminar rooms are located in the administrative area and adjacent to the library.

Library

The library at the New Leith Academy is a shared-access facility, designed for both public and school use. The design supports private study and open learning. Computer rooms have been designated for student and adult use. Other areas in the library include: printing/reprographics unit, dark room, graphics studio, audio/video resource production facility, and hardware maintenance area with secure storage.

Other areas designated for shared-use by the public include: business studies area, gymnasium, swimming pool, and the café. Some facilities have been created specifically for community use, including a nursery and the community lounge.

Services in the science labs are supplied by flexible hoses.

Furniture Design

Furniture design is one aspect of the school's effort to be adaptable to changing needs. The architects chose a "loose-fit" approach in designing the furnishings. In keeping with the overall design approach, they developed a modular furniture system composed of removable desktops supported by metal "C" frames. The frames provide for low (700 mm) and high (900 mm) work surfaces. Loose under bench cupboards provide storage space. These components are easily moveable and interchangeable.

KEY POINTS

- A modular system of design is applied at all scales of the building which allows for ease of planning, design and future flexibility.

- Design goals include flexibility and a strategy to accommodate changes in the number of students served.

- An internal street is used as an organizing principle and to promote energy efficient design.

- The design promotes concurrent community and school use.

- New Leith Academy uses information technology extensively throughout the building and has planned for increased use.

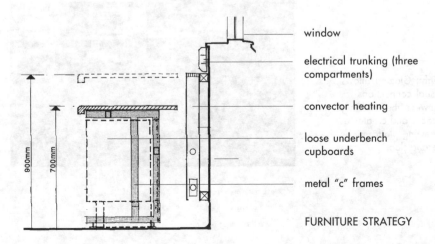

window

electrical trunking (three compartments)

convector heating

loose underbench cupboards

metal "c" frames

FURNITURE STRATEGY

The architects designed a modular furniture system that allows adaptation to a range of situations.

Right: Immanuel Technology Center: exterior view of the electronics and robotics workshop.

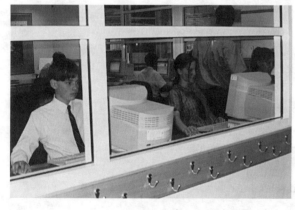

Above: Students work in the materials workshop.

Right: Glazing allows visual connections between the workshop spaces and creates a "viewing platform" on the second floor.

Immanuel College Technology Centre

Adelaide, Australia

The Technology Centre at Immanuel College is thought to be one of the most advanced in Australia. Immanuel College is an independent, coeducational secondary school with 750 students. Mr. Jacobi was a member of the core writing team for Australia's Technology Curriculum Project. The building's design and use reflects his thinking about the direction of education with information technology.

Architect: Geof Nairn Architects
Completed: 1993
Budget: A$1.2 million

CURRICULUM GOALS

The Centre's curriculum is based on Australia's National Statement on Technology Education which specifies three interrelated components - materials, information and systems. An understanding of the relationship between the three areas is as important as the understanding of each area of concentration. The curriculum has a clear link to industry and particularly computer-based manufacturing, a predominant industry in South Australia.

Compressed air, gas, water and electricity are provided at the hexoganal tables in the controls lab.

The objective of the materials component is to develop an understanding of the properties and exploration of the limits of materials. Information technology is used for design and modeling leading to application and evaluation. The systems component explores the use of information technology in controlling industrial processes (and assuring quality). These processes include: electronics, mechanics, pneumatics, and microelectronics. These three areas: materials, information and systems are intended to be interrelated through design.

The overall curriculum objectives are to develop transferable skills and knowledge which are relevant to other subject areas, and inspire creative work. Students learn methods of problem solving through design, assembly and testing. Technology is demystified with hands on investigation and creative thinking. Student collaboration is seen as an important aspect of this approach. Students work independently and together to solve problems and investigate new ideas.

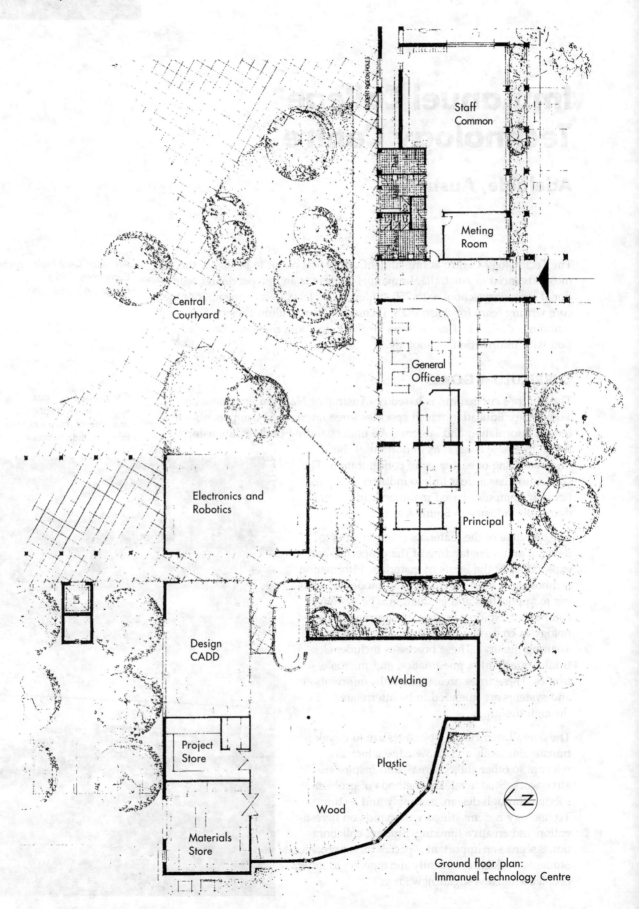

Staff
Common

Meting
Room

Central
Courtyard

General
Offices

Principal

Electronics and
Robotics

Design
CADD

Welding

Lift

Project
Store

Plastic

Wood

Materials
Store

Ground floor plan:
Immanuel Technology Centre

Students at work in the materials workshop.

BUILDING DESIGN

Immanuel's Technology Centre supports the learning activities of the larger campus. The building required careful site planning to integrate with the existing campus structures. A separate entry and independent building was designed to allow for extended use of the building for industry and community use, for teacher training and for use as a conference center. Included in the project is an addition to the existing campus library. An emphasis of the project was to carefully match the building design's with appropriate services, natural light and acoustic controls. Mr. Jacobi stressed that the building should send a message that this was an important learning environment for all students, including female students. The goal was to create an environment which was highly adaptable for many types of activities. The organization of each workshop is intended to enhance cooperative learning with students working in teams or in pairs at the hexagonal tables. Emphasizing connection between various work/study areas, glazed partitions provide views between most of the rooms. This also allows for ease of supervision, and greater independence for the students. The Centre includes a suite of four workshops located on two floors, including materials, CAD Area, Electronics and Robotics, and Multimedia.

The largest workshop is the materials area with work benches for wood, plastics, metal and other materials work. Computer-controlled manufacturing equipment will gradually be introduced to this area. The materials room is brightly lit, almost free of columns. The materials storage is directly adjacent to the workroom. In addition, a project storage room is provided for storage of ongoing student work.

In the computer-aided design workshop, the workstations are located around the perimeter of the room.

The Computer Aided Design (CAD) room is adjacent to the materials room. Computers are organized for ease of access, to electrical service and networking along the perimeter of the wall. Hexagonal work tables are provided in the center of the room. The multimedia room is located directly above the CAD room on the second level, and is similarly organized.

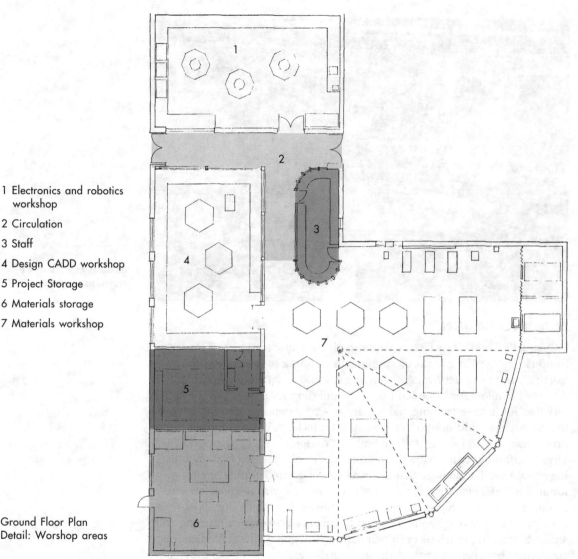

1 Electronics and robotics
   workshop
2 Circulation
3 Staff
4 Design CADD workshop
5 Project Storage
6 Materials storage
7 Materials workshop

Ground Floor Plan
Detail: Worshop areas

Glazing provides a visual
connection between the
Design Workshop and the
Materials Workshop.

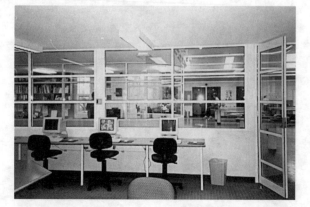

The electronics and robotics room is a double-height space with a barrel vault roof form. It is serviced with compressed air, gas and electricity at work tables. The perimeter of the room provides work bench space for specific equipment and storage.

INFORMATION TECHNOLOGY

Information technology is located in the design workshop (CAD Room) and Multimedia room. Each contains 20 computer workstations. Not every student is intended to be working at the computer at the same time, as multiple activities take place within the Centre. Additional computers are located in the extended library, in specialist teaching areas and in two additional computing areas located separately amongst the classrooms throughout the campus.

In past years, the initial supply of equipment was supported through price discounting provided by the suppliers. In addition the establishment of an equipment leasing program enables the College to turn the hardware over at regular intervals within the cost of the initial investment. This policy was commonly found at the school sites visited in Australia. In this way, schools were able to provide up-to-date equipment. This policy has changed, increasing the cost of maintaining an inventory of up-to-date equipment. Immanuel has chosen to lease computers both to provide the latest equipment for the students and to reduce maintenance costs for the equipment.

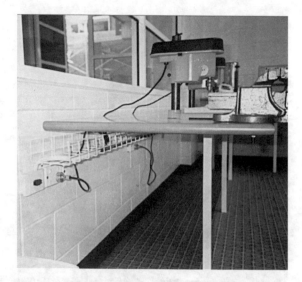

Cable trays around the perimeter of the room allow for power and network cabling.

The building was not networked initially, but ducting for cabling was included in the design. Within the first year of operation however, demand made it clear that the network was required, and the network will be provided throughout the school. As the rooms have been designed with perimeter cable trays below the work bench, it should not be too difficult to install the network cabling. The first stage of networking has been completed in May, 1994. A satellite dish and antenna currently allows for the reception of weather satellite information.

Links with Industry

The Centre has also received industry sponsorship. The link to industry is important from a curriculum perspective, as well as a financial perspective. Reflecting a changing role for educational buildings with information technology, the Centre is appropriately designed to train teachers and parents, in addition to training students. The Centre is also used as a training centre for industry.

KEY POINTS

- Purpose built design to match requirements of Technology Curriculum.
- Independent building for use for teacher training, parents and industry workshops as well as students.
- Adaptable design includes design of furnishings and networking cable distribution.

The Materials Workshop is the largest of the areas in the Technology Centre.

Above right and left: "Ground Level" (upper level) opens onto to the school yard. Note the distinctive curve of the bowstring truss roof.

Right: "Focus Pavillions are located in the nodal areas linking buildings.

Above Left: Steps at lower ground level lead to the main complex.

Cherrybrook Technology High School

Sydney, Australia

The Cherrybrook Technology High School is the one of 28 purpose built schools designated as technology focus schools in the State of New South Wales, Australia. The curriculum at all the technology high schools emphasizes "the study of the application of scientific and other knowledge in relation to practical tasks". Learning about technology is intended to be integrated throughout the curriculum.

Cherrybrook is designed to create a flexible and adaptable environment able to respond to changes in teaching methods, use of technology and educational program. The image of the building is intended to reflect the emphasis on technology within the school.

A large staff "study" (or teachers' common work area) is provided to bring the entire teaching staff together and to support team teaching. The building organization offers a range of opportunities to students to access information technology: within the classroom, adjacent to computer study areas, in computer learning spaces, and at the information centre. The building is fully networked. The building's structure and partition system allows for re-configuration of classrooms and other learning spaces. Design and construction was "fast-tracked" to provide for a shortened construction schedule, and for ongoing design decisions.

New Construction
Occupied: 1992
Architect: Public Works Departments' "Schools Architects" and Department of Schools Education
Number of students: 900
(note: in 1994 the student number is 1059 and in 1995, enrollment will exceed 1100)

TEACHING AND LEARNING

At Cherrybrook, information technology is viewed as a "tool for learning" as well as being the focus of specialized studies within the total curriculum. Each student studies "Design and Technology" in at least one year. The philosophy of integrating technology throughout the curriculum, is intended to be reinforced by the students "seeing the staff and administration use the same technology in the running of the school".

The principal and two senior staff were selected a full year prior to the opening of the school in an effort to insure the success of the program. The faculty selected were considered "risk takers" rather than technocrats and had a positive attitude toward new teaching methods. The aim was to build teams within the teaching staff with a mix of strengths. Experience using information technology in teaching was not a selection criterion, rather the teacher's commitment to learn to use technology was paramount. The school is organized to bring the teaching staff together to work cooperatively, to develop the curriculum and to continue the learning process.

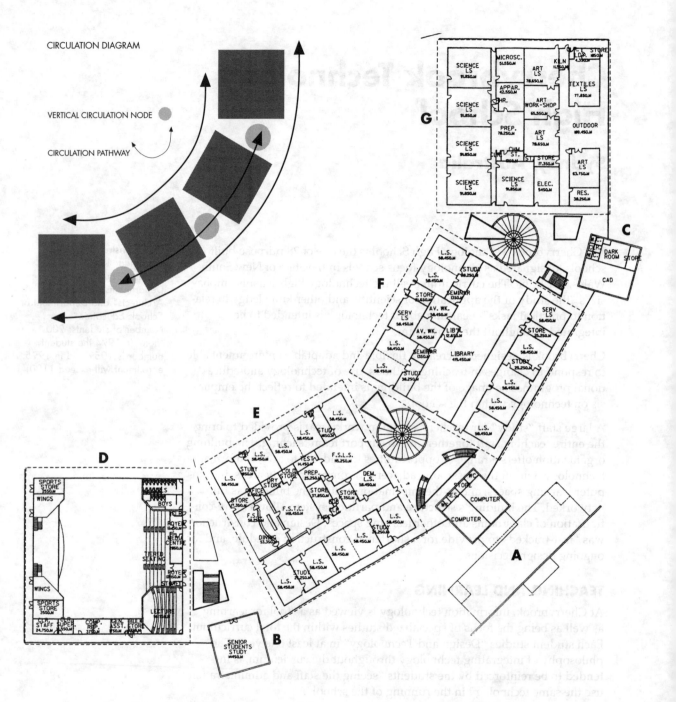

CIRCULATION DIAGRAM

VERTICAL CIRCULATION NODE

CIRCULATION PATHWAY

Ground Floor Plan
(upper floor)

A   Administration/Computer
B   Senior Students Study
C   Design Centre
D   Multipurpose Centre, Lecture
    Theatre, Media Centre
E   General Learning – Food
    Technology/Music/Languages
F   Library/General Learning
G   Science/Art/Industrial Technology

BUILDING DESIGN

The school building complex forms a crescent-shaped plan on a sloped site. It comprises four separate structures, which house the "technology centres", plus an administration building which serves as the entry gate to the complex. The steel frame buildings are designed with bowstring truss roofs to provide for clear spans within which provide maximum flexibility. The design takes advantage of the change in elevation offering outdoor access at two levels: "lower ground level" (public) and "ground level" (private school yard). "Focus Pavilions" are located at the nodes between the four buildings.

The design for the complex allows for ease of circulation through covered exterior walkways, interior corridors and covered exterior stairways located at the "Focus Pavilions". The bowstring truss roofs extend over the exterior circulation paths to provide protection from sun and rain. Most rooms exit directly to the outdoors. This circulation pattern helps integrate interior and exterior for educational use, one benefit of the warm climate.

The upper level contains the majority of the learning spaces including those for general science and art instruction, as well as the library. Specialized technology labs including the computer aided design (CADD), textiles, food technology, multimedia, and electronics labs are located on the upper level. The lower level houses a multi-purpose hall and facilities for music and language as well as the staff study. Industrial work shops, and the robotics and graphics labs are also located at the lower level.

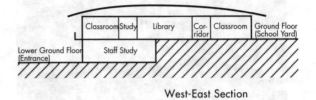

West-East Section

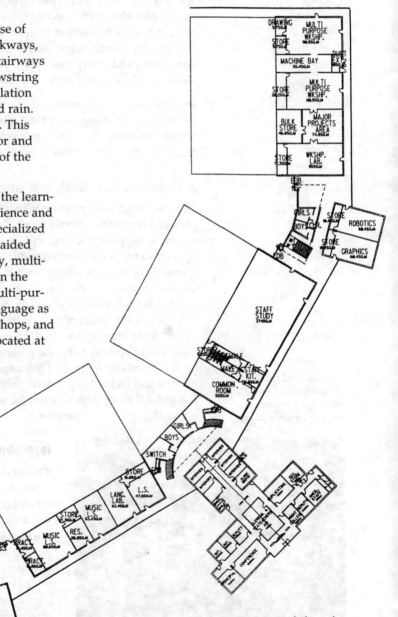

Lower Ground Floor Plan

Students work together in CAD lab.

Classroom Organization

The use of the bowstring truss roof supported by the exterior walls creates structurally unencumbered space within each building. Each building can be one completely open space or subdivided into "classrooms" or other learning areas. These learning areas can be reconfigured to respond to changing educational methods, curriculum and use of technology.

The interior classroom walls and partitions are non-load bearing, permitting flexibility in configuring the interior space. Classrooms can be reorganized with metal stud partitions, demountable partitions or movable walls. These three wall types create a range of choices for possible alterations. Movable walls can be 'opened' by the teacher on an "as need basis", the positioning of demountable walls can alter the dimension of a space within a few hours, while alteration of the stud walls requires a more time consuming and costly renovation process. Electric power and networking are located at the exterior wall or accessed through the ceiling.

In some cases this flexibility is restricted by the provision of electric service. An unforeseen change was the redesign of a microscopy science area into a media computer lab. Access to electric power at the perimeter lab benches made for an easy transition from science lab to media center.

Administration Building and Staff Study

The administration building is located front and center of the school complex as a figurative "front door." The teachers' staff study room was designed to support teaching with information technology. The large open-plan room clusters individual work spaces. Teachers' desks are grouped together by subject area to allow collaboration and interaction. Cross-discipline interaction is also possible within this open-office environment. The Staff Study is equipped with computer workstations on movable carts which the teachers share although the teachers would prefer individual computers at this time. The teaching staff is enthusiastic about the "staff study" concept and the ability to work together. The staff study has been particularly helpful as teachers accept the challenge of teaching with information technology. Interestingly enough, the success of the staff study has made it more desirable for the administrators to be closer to the teaching staff in the main complex.

Facilities and resources are centralized in the Staff Study promoting teacher communication.

INFORMATION TECHNOLOGY

The school is fully wired with a local area network. All services have been concentrated in a service corridor beneath the complex. The network distribution is primarily through the hung ceilings along the corridors or through the exterior walls. Within the classrooms and computer labs, networking and power is distributed with use of trunking or specific access points depending on frequency of use. At a minimum, each classroom is provided with at least one data port. Seventy-five per cent of the classrooms also include a video port. Some classrooms have been designed with raised floors (or double floors) in those rooms with intensive use of information technology such as the language instruction area. Within the library, power poles provide flexible access to power and networking.

The school operates on a uniform platform with IBM computers. IBM Australia is one of the major sponsors of the school. In 1993, there were approximate 300 computers for 860 students. Cherrybrook has developed mutually supportive links with a number of businesses which contribute equipment and expertise to the school.

Information technology as a tool for learning is found throughout the school. The technology centres provide a one-to-one student-to-computer ratio, while computer workstations are provided as required in classrooms. Small technology resource centers are also located between classrooms. The library serves as the main distribution point for portable computers for student and teacher use, as well as for other portable equipment such as video players and monitors. Within the staff study, teachers share networked computers located on movable carts.

Students in all years are comfortable using the library.

PARTNERSHIP WITH INDUSTRY

Cherrybrook High School is the result of a partnership between the community, industry and the Department of Schools and Education. The design was developed by the State Public Works Department. A key aspect of the project was maximizing private sector input. The designers credit this collaboration as well as a fast-track construction process for delivering an on-time and on-budget school taking 18 months to construct. The business sector provided some sponsorship for the school and IBM provided input into its design (particularly in the network design). The resulting facility offers several community resources including a multi-purpose center for community use, a drama and dance theater and a conference facility.

KEY POINTS

- Cherrybrook High School is dedicated to the integration of technology into the curriculum; information technology as a tool for learning is located throughout the school.

- The school is designed as a group of four main buildings which provide a light-filled environment and activate the use of exterior spaces.

- Interior partition walls can be reconfigured to allow for reorganization of classroom and other learning spaces over time.

- The staff study brings the entire teaching staff together providing each teacher with personal work-space, access to computers and opportunity for collaborative work and sharing.

- Network cabling is provided throughout the school with data and video ports in each room. Distribution of cable is primarily through ceilings along corridors.

- There is a 3:1 student to computer ratio operating on an IBM pc platform.

Above left and right:
Kawasaki City High
School features two types
of computer lab
arrangements.

Right: Axonometric
drawing shows the
relationship between the
two existing school
buildings, built in 1961
and 1962, and the new
tower and gymnasium,
built in 1991.

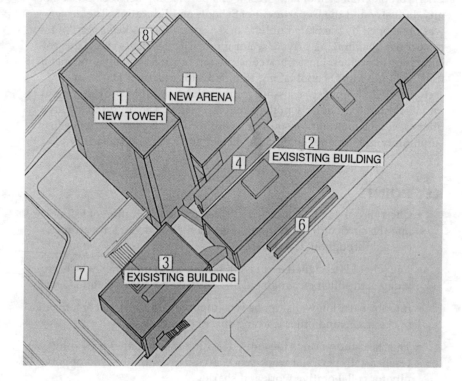

8

1
NEW ARENA

1
NEW TOWER

4

2
EXISISTING BUILDING

6

7

3
EXISISTING BUILDING

Kawasaki City High School for Science and Technology

Kawasaki, Japan

Kawasaki City High School for Science and Technology is a new 16-story addition to an existing vocational school building. Opened in 1991, the total planned capacity of the school is 800 students. Located in one of the most industrial cities in Japan, this high-rise building (the tallest high school building in Japan) is intended to be a symbolic gate to the city.

Kawasaki City High School integrates the use of information technology in both the vocational educational program and the building management. The school was developed by the city to create an educational program and a facility that would complement the city's technology-based industry. The project was initiated at a time when there was a profound need to support and address the changing requirement for vocational education. This need continues throughout Japan today. The nature of industrial work in Kawasaki has changed from traditionally 50 percent blue collar to 80 percent research employment.

The school is the result of six years of planning. As a measure of its success, focus will be placed on the ability of Kawasaki's graduating students to find employment in business and industry and their ability to excel in their placements. However, students have already won awards for academic and creative achievement.

CURRICULUM: Change in Vocational Education

One of the key goals for the design of the Kawasaki City High School's educational program was to examine the needs of students entering industry and to address those needs within vocational education training. Information technology was identified by the planning committee as an important element in this program. Their vision was to create a new environment that would both meet changing requirements and would inspire students in vocational education. The main goal was to provide a vocational educational program that would be competitive with the best educational programs in Kawasaki. The curriculum was designed to address a problem facing many educators world-wide: the need to offer students an interesting and relevant curriculum.

The original Kawasaki Technical High School was founded in the mid 1960s providing education primarily in "sub-manufacturing." The committee wanted to change the image of the school and offer a forward-thinking educational program in order to encourage more students to consider vocational education.

This goal was accomplished through several approaches. First the name of the school was changed to the Kawasaki City High School for Science and Technology from Kawasaki City Technical High School. This signaled a change away from the "3-D's," "Dark, Dirty and Dangerous," associated

New Construction and Renovation

Senior High School

Occupied: 1991

Number of students: 800

Building area: 31 000 m²

Construction costs: US$120 Million

Architect:
MHS Planners, Architects & Engineers

An important goal for the new high school was to increase female enrollment.

with vocational education. This symbolic shift was followed by a change in the curriculum which added information technology, science and design. While traditional vocational education courses such as electronics were continued, some courses were eliminated. Rather than focusing solely on skill-based learning, the curriculum was designed to strengthen "academic" learning, for example, foreign languages and higher math. Another step was to encourage more female students into the program. Approximately 20 percent of the enrollment is now female, and 75 percent of design students are female.

Creating a connection between the students at the school and industry was a key goal. In Japan, much vocational training is conducted within the workplace or within industry training centers. This is the case for large companies. Smaller companies, however, cannot afford the expense of worker training and rely on the vocational schools. Therefore, the vocational school must demonstrate relevance to the workplace. For this reason, more teachers were selected from industry, who could draw upon their workplace experience.

Community Use and Life Long Learning

The school was also intended to be a resource to the community and to support "life long learning" activities. The community has access to the library and a community center from 10 a.m. to 8 p.m. The library is equipped with computers and custom designed VCR booths for community use. The fully networked facility allows community members to access data bases both nationally and internationally. Each community member will pay a fee for access to data resources based on a use.

BUILDING DESIGN

The school combines the renovation of two five-story structures, built in 1961 and 1962, with a newly constructed 16-story high-rise classroom tower and a new gymnasium. The new tower is organized into four zones: library; administration; classrooms; and computer science, with a dining area on the top floor. The facility also includes a television recording studio. The roof houses the air conditioning plant and a heliport for evacuation.

VCR booths located in the library are made available for public use.

The design intention was to create an alternative image for the vocational education school which has too often been designed to resemble a factory. Instead, the facility has been generally designed like an office building with a large impressive ground floor lobby and floors above that allow for a flexible plan.

The classroom tower houses all of the school's academic departments. Each department occupies a single floor and is composed of a prep room, a teaching materials room, a lecture classroom, other classrooms and, in the case of natural sciences, a laboratory.

The floor plan is organized as a simple double-loaded corridor. Demountable walls free from the structural column grid allow all walls to be moved and reorganized. In this way, some of the learning areas can be traditional classrooms, while others can be large spaces with landscape office furnishings and large student work tables. Use of interior glazing from the corridor to the classrooms is intended to open the classrooms to one another.

As a demonstration of education with information technology, different types and configurations of computer lab organizations are included in the facility. Some of these lab settings promote collaborative learning while others are organized in "lecture format." There are 42 computer workstations provided in each class. Students are allowed access to the building for studying and to use the computer labs until 8 p.m.

The lower part of the building, which includes the library, has been used for the school's community functions. A computer system is used to manage the more than 10,000 volumes in the school's library. Students can check books in and out of the library themselves with the use of a bar code reader and their identification card.

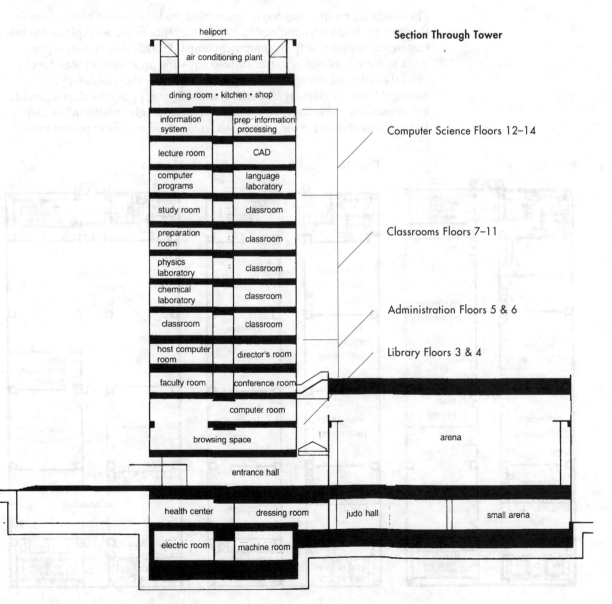

Section Through Tower

Computer Science Floors 12–14

Classrooms Floors 7–11

Administration Floors 5 & 6

Library Floors 3 & 4

Students check out books from the library themselves using a bar code scanner.

INFORMATION TECHNOLOGY

The school has been developed to take full advantage of information technology. The 12th, 13th and 14th floors are organized for use of teaching and learning with information technology. For this reason, raised floor (double floors) have been provided to allow for flexibility in networking. The building is fully networked with fiber optic cable and two local area networks, one for administration and one for academic purposes.

Support from Industry

As the city of Kawasaki is one of the nation's major industrial centers, industry partnerships supported the design of the new vocational school. Several international corporations are located within the community and have contributed to the development of the school.

The design committee wanted to assure that students would have access to the most up-to-date technology to insure relevance to the workplace. For this reason, the suggestion from computer companies that they donate equipment to the school was rejected. Instead a leasing arrangement was developed that allowed the school to upgrade and renew the equipment on a biannual basis. In this way, the school could stay at pace with developments in information technology. At the same time, no single "platform" or manufacturer was chosen for the school. Students would receive exposure to a

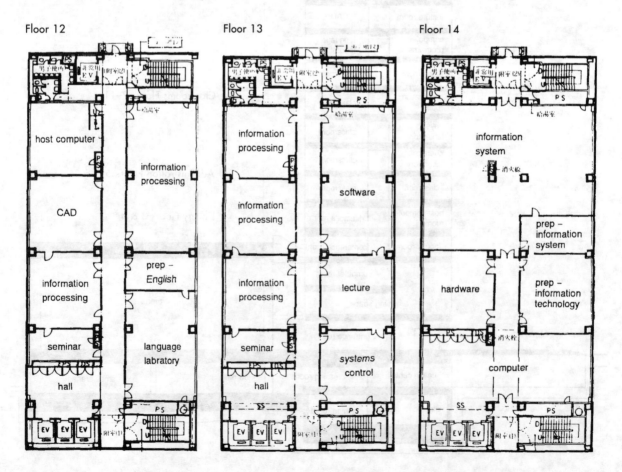

Floor 12   Floor 13   Floor 14

broad range of types of computer equipment. The committee felt that students would learn more and gain an appreciation for the characteristics of the computer by comparison. Contributors to the school include: SUN, IBM, Apple Computers, Fujitsu, Toshiba and NEC.

Intelligent Building

The design of the "intelligent" building makes use of the network to control and monitor building systems from a central computer, including heating, ventilation, air conditioning, elevator control, electric power, lighting, security, and fire protection systems. Each floor in the tower has

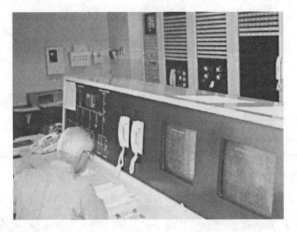

Kawasaki High School's building systems are centrally controlled in an "intelligent building" model.

been independently zoned so environmental systems can be shut down when a department is not in use. Swipe ID cards are used by students to gain access to certain areas of the facility, allowing controlled access and monitoring of use. The intelligent system also allows for the development of a database on the use and performance of the building's systems supporting building management decision-making.

Cost

The facility was twice as expensive as a typical educational building, costing US$120 million. The increased cost can be attributed to the intelligent building function, structural cost of the high-rise facility, building details, and other features such as the heliport on the roof. Half the funds were raised by local bond and half came from the general budget of the city of Kawasaki. This extra cost was justified in the Kawasaki City Congress with the condition that it be opened to the community.

KEY POINTS

- Kawasaki City High School represents a change from the negative perception of vocational education to a positive, central role.

- The use of information technology is fully integrated in both the educational program and building management.

- Industry partnerships supported the design of the new vocational school and contributed to its development.

- The new 16-story addition to an existing vocational school building has been generally designed like an office building.

- "Intelligent building" allows for monitoring and control of heating, ventilation, lighting, security and fire protection from a central location.

- The building has been designed for flexibility with demountable walls free from the structural column grid and a raised floor for cable management.

- The school provides community resources to support "life long learning."

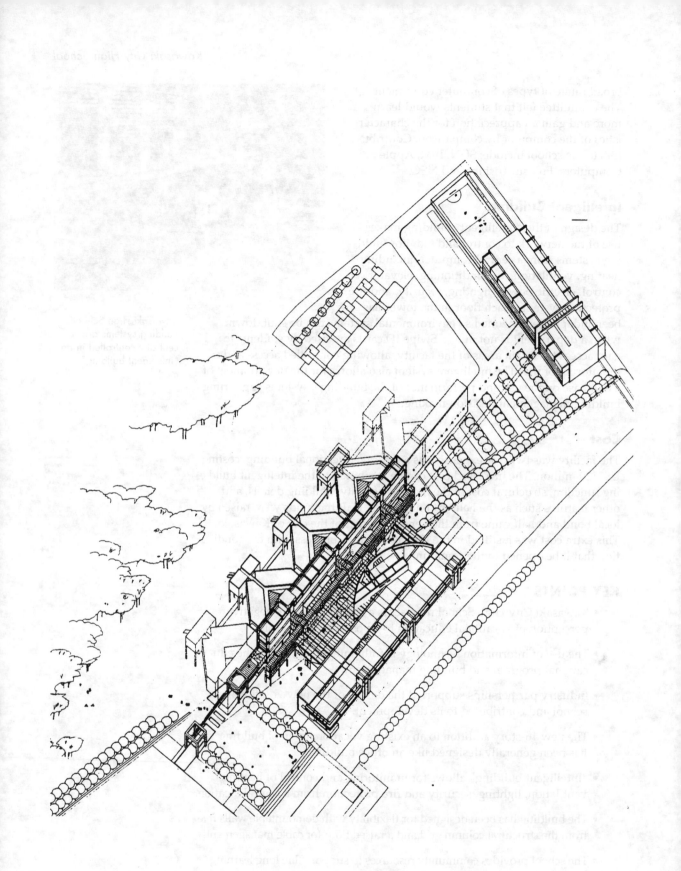

Axonometric view

Lycée Marie Curie

Echirolles, France

The Lycée Marie Curie was designed to introduce new information technology into education and to implement changes in pedagogical practice, including greater use of individual and small group work. The school was developed through a collaborative effort involving parents, educators, architects and planners. Since the successful completion of this project, the community has continued on to develop the "College of the Future" which incorporates many of the ideas learned through the development of Lycée Marie Curie. The College is located in a "new town" close to Grenoble in the southeast of France. Many of France's software developers and information technology companies have located their enterprises in the Grenoble area. The school's design was intended to provide an educational environment for the community and business, as well as traditional students.

Perhaps one of the most important aspects of Lycée Marie Curie was the multi-disciplinary design process which involved educators, administrators, architects, technology experts and planners. The goal of the school was to develop an educational setting for collaboration between teachers and students. Three types of educational areas were envisioned for the school: (1) theoretical and practical learning areas, (2) management and control areas linked to other sectors, and (3) the public or intermediate areas.

BUILDING DESIGN

The building plan is organized with a glazed central court called 'the Agora' which provides circulation to public and administrative spaces as well as educational areas. One of the key features of the building was to promote student interaction and student learning beyond the classroom. The 1000 square meter, double-height space is intended to be an area for students to meet and exchange information. The Agora is intended to be a setting for expositions and information. In addition to this large public space, other smaller informal meeting spaces are found throughout the school.

The administrative area and teachers' rooms are located adjacent to the Agora near the entrance, symbolically, as the "brains" of the school. Other public function spaces are located adjacent to the Agora, including the restaurant or cafeteria. A large covered ground floor terrace is provided to allow for possible future expansion of the school as required.

Five types of learning areas are included: (1) classrooms, (2) computer labs, (3) multimedia center and (4) science labs and (5) language labs. Overall, the building plan focuses on appropriate adjacencies, or the relationship of learning spaces to one another, as well as the need to create a networked, adaptable building. The building is organized with parallel corridors with glazed roofs to bring natural light deep into the building.

Secondary School
New Construction
Occupied: 1991
Architect: Groupe Six
Number of Students:
1680
Building area: 1800 M
Cost: 100,000,000 FF
without taxes (18%)
studies (8%) or equipment

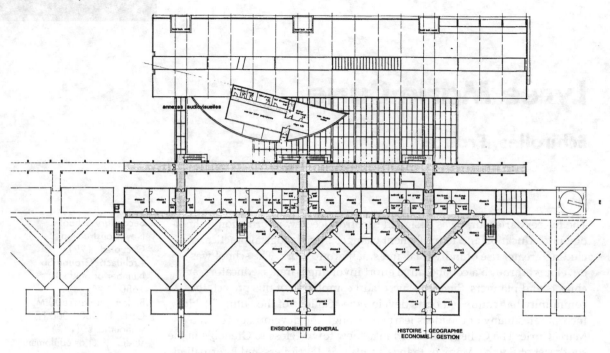

Plan View

Multimedia Center

The multimedia center is located on the first floor of the building to allow for use of the center after school hours. The center functions as a library with print media and also provides access to equipment including CD Roms, networked computer workstations, and video players. Students are able to access data bases and networks within the media center. The center is designed with raised floors (or double floors) for flexible placement and re-arrangement of computer work stations. Several glazed, acoustically attenuated booths are provided for use of video equipment, video disks and audio tapes. The multimedia center is designed for many types of groups to work and study: the individual, the teacher, small groups and a full class.

Top: Raised floors are included in areas of intensive use of computers such as the Media Center.

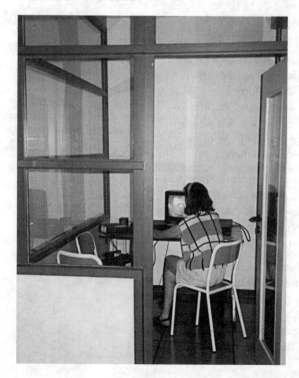

Classrooms

The classrooms are organized for lecture format. All classrooms are networked and have at least one large screen monitor, video player and a networked computer. Custom designed, lockable storage units house this equipment for security purposes and ease of use. In classrooms designated for use of computers, the classrooms have raised floors to allow for distribution of network cabling and electric power.

Computer Lab

The computer labs are found in proximity to the classrooms as a resource for student use, and for instructional purposes. These labs have raised floors. The computer labs are located on the interior of the building with large windows, looking onto the Agora. In this way the labs can benefit from "borrowed light" from the court and avoid the potential for glare from direct sunlight. At the same time they are highly visible spaces to "invite" the students.

Science Lab

The science labs are integrated with computer workstations and an access port to the network at each lab bench. An important feature of the science lab is the shared teachers' prep area which is designed to be a collaborative working environment. The generous work space allows the instructors to work together to develop their curriculum. This room was considered particularly important as instructors embarked on the difficult task of developing a new curriculum and methods of teaching with information technology.

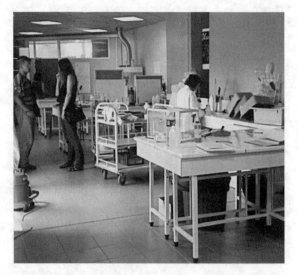

Above: Shared teacher preparation area promotes exchange between teachers.

INFORMATION TECHNOLOGY

One of the primary goals in the implementation of the technology program was that the system allow for change over time. A fiber optic backbone is used to network the building, with a secondary distribution to classrooms with twisted-pair copper wire. The network is centrally controlled. All computers may access data base resources in the library. A raised floor system was used in computer labs, corridors, the library and some classrooms. In other rooms, the networking is achieved through wall mounted trunking. To date, the computer rooms have already been altered four times. In addition, each classroom is equipped with a lockable computer cabinet, large screen monitor, video player and computer to access the network. The lecture hall is equipped with a three color projector that is used by students to present their work.

While the design and organization of the school have been used as a model, three concerns have been identified for both the Lycée and the newly planned "College of the Future": (1) increased cost which is attributed to design features, cabling and additional space due to added program, (2) added requirements placed on the teaching faculty to develop innovative teaching programs and (3) the need for better climate control.

KEY POINTS

- The building plan is organized around a central agora intended for student demonstration and exchange of ideas.
- Building-wide network and raised floors within computer labs, classrooms and the media center.
- Media center is designed for community and school use with spaces designed for use of information technology.
- Every classroom includes a networked computer, monitor and video player housed in lockable storage unit.
- Faculty and administrative spaces are designed as important components of the school's ongoing development.
- An area of the building is designated for industry training and community use.
- The building is designed to allow for ongoing expansion.

Above: Exterior view of Merksworth High School

Above right: Power pole is used to access network cables and electric power in Business Lab

Right: Students work in Technology Lab with sufficient territory to organize work in addition to working at the computer work station.

Merksworth High School Hi-Tech Centre

Paisley, Strathclyde Region, Scotland

Many "schools of the future" are characterized by a select enrollment and newly constructed building. This is a school for all students. Merksworth High School made use of an existing building to promote a technology-based education as a vehicle for social and economic growth. The Strathclyde Regional Council has made a major commitment to a social strategy focusing on social and economic regeneration and equal opportunities. The building design, as well as the curriculum design, encourages and facilitates the use of the Hi-Tech Centre by young people and adults with special educational needs.

The Strathclyde Regional Council wanted to increase opportunities in a community with three generations of unemployment, serving both students and their parents. This school is supported by the local business community. Rather than constructing a new school, the Council funded the renovation a 1973 school building that had been subject to vandalism and neglect. The program and the building at Merksworth High School were designed to meet the needs of several groups: students and adults, local industry and the community as a whole.

Many difficulties arise in a community that suffers from generations of unemployment. Often students and their parents question the value of education when they see limited prospects for employment. In creating a technology-rich curriculum Merksworth High School hopes to break this cycle of unemployment and to increase opportunities by preparing students to play important roles in a rapidly changing and technologically oriented world.

One of the major industries in this area (Renfrewshire) is the production of information technology equipment. The export of this equipment is an important contribution to Scotland's net export market and a significant percentage of information technology equipment in the world market.

TEACHING AND LEARNING

Merksworth offers a flexible technology and business based curriculum with elective modules or courses. All students receive individualized instruction during their first two years through tutoring sessions. Modules respond to the changing needs of students, and to reflect advances in technology. Merksworth has found that new modules need to be introduced every year and that the majority of current courses were not taught three years ago.

Technology education at Merksworth features electronics, computer aided design and manufacturing, robotics, communications and programmable systems. Technology courses are organized into three categories based on

Renovation/Retrofit
Ages 11-18
Architect: David Gray, Director
Department of Architecture and Related Services
Strathclyde Regional Council
Occupied: 1991

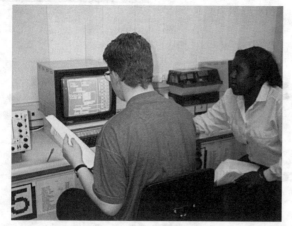

Teachers work as a tutors or coaches, in an "as needed" basis. Here a student teacher works with a student who attends Merksworth once a week, as a visiting student from another school.

students' previous experience. Many courses require no previous experience, while other courses require pre-requisite skills or knowledge. Business education at Merksworth focuses on two areas: information technology in commerce and office technology. All courses use Macintosh and PC compatible computers and electronic data transmission equipment. Computer data processing, with emphasis on the understanding of computer systems and application software are addressed in commerce courses. Office technology courses focus on the organization of technologically advanced office skills required for work.

Music

Music curriculum at Merksworth is designed for vocation training as well as enrichment. Midi technology used within the music suite is extremely popular with the students. The educators believe that music can provide insights into other areas of study, such as drama, physics, English, and computing. The curriculum is designed for both the novice and the experienced musician. All instruction is individualized to respond to students needs. Students can earn SCOTVEC (Scottish Vocational Education Certificates) in Music Composition and in Music Production and Sound Engineering.

Tutorial Center

Often students attending Merksworth are not prepared with the necessary skills to succeed in this technology-based learning environment. The Merksworth curricula counters this problem with a tutoring program. Key to the success of the program, all students receive tutoring one afternoon per week for their first two years. Sessions are spent addressing a student's individual needs or pursuing a project of special interest.

Further Education

Merksworth provides a valuable resource to the community by offering education to adults. At the same time, the building's overall efficiency is increased by extending the use of facility and its equipment. Merksworth Centre includes an extended learning program offering specialized courses for schools, industry and the Paisley area community. Current courses include: computer graphics, CAD/CAM, electronics, biotechnology, business, European languages, music, drama and theatre arts. Special provisions have been made to make adults feel welcome at the school. For instance, a special adult lounge has been furnished. Merksworth High School also provides a valuable opportunity for visiting students. Its courses and its technology-rich environment attract students enrolled at other schools for the balance of their curricular choices.

Industry Partnership

Merksworth's goal is to ensure that students are prepared to enter into the job market. As industry in the Strathclyde Region has become increasingly technology-based, the new curriculum reflects this trend. The school has developed partnerships with industry and business. Merksworth brings business, and the community into the school by offering a wide variety of relevant courses and by making its facilities available for conferences, business meetings and community use.

Adjacent to the controls area is the design area with computer workstations for CAD design and computer programming. Note that work space is left open for students to draw, and work with paper and pencil as well as the computer. Students work together and individually in this space.

BUILDING DESIGN

The Merksworth building is a four-story building with a traditional double-loaded corridor plan. The technology suite, was created through minimal alterations to the existing building such as removing some walls and adding new partitions, carpeting and ceilings.

The school's renovation focused on specific educational spaces, those that would benefit the most from an infusion of technology. This approach was due to a limited budget, and in part, to a decline in the size of the enrollment. The overall plan of the school remained unchanged. The low cost renovation included the development of a networking system for the entire school.

The technology suite includes: (1) the technology lab, (2) the business lab and (3) graphics design. Other technology based rooms located throughout the building include: the media rooms, the music room and the tutorial center.

Students work in the controls area in the technology lab. The design of this area includes appropriate, and well-organized storage for tools.

The Technology Lab is designed with two areas. Students learn the principles of electronics by designing, building and testing their own electronic devices in the controls area. The other area is for computer programming and computer aided design. Specialized furnishings form the work area along the perimeter of the room. The specialized trunking supplies services needed for electronics or robotics such as soldering and compressed air. This trunking also provides power and networking connections. The room is neat, open and includes the use of bright colors to give an aesthetically exciting environment at a low cost.

The Business Lab is arranged to recreate a technologically advanced office. Services, including power and networking, are provided by regularly spaced power poles. The cable management is organized through the furniture to receptacles located at the same height as the work surface. The desks can be moved and are currently arranged in groups of four centered on each power pole. Additional work surfaces are located in the center of the room and along the perimeter.

The graphic design area focuses on the use of computing equipment and design software that could be found in business. The graphic design area is organized with perimeter desks surrounding a large work table. The central table can be used for student discussions, layout work, design and instruction.

The school includes a simple recording studio for video. The recording studio has been created with use of an existing classroom. All the editing equipment is located on movable carts for flexibility.

NETWORK DISTRIBUTION

The technology suite renovation provided perimeter trunking that supplies power and networking services. In some instances, rooms were also equipped with power poles to provide additional service connections and allow for greater flexibility in arrangement of furniture within the room. Most furniture is modular and can be rearranged or redistributed to meet changing requirements. Computer hardware is also modular and can be reallocated if necessary.

Graphics Lab

The Media Room is a very simple classroom with equipment located on movable carts.

KEY POINTS

- With limited funds and thoughtful renovations, Merksworth has created an effective, technology-rich learning environment.

- Although full-time student enrollment is low relative to the size of the building, efficiency has been increased by extending the building's use to include further education and business functions.

- Curriculum and technology are flexible. Each is designed to reflect changes in industry and society.

- The school is designed for both secondary students and adult use. The educational program teaches skills required to work in the information technology industries within the area to help improve the local economy and the welfare of the community.

There are strong messages throughout the building that this is a place of learning, signals that trigger the 'want' to learn. . . . (Students) don't need to feel alienated, there is no need to react against it, that this is very special and in a way that they are privileged to be here. This is what we've got to get across to people, not that the second rate is good enough for you, but that you are good enough for the best. (Nick Brown, Principal)

Top: Entrance

Middle: Computer Resource area

Lower: Students work together on group project.

Oldham Sixth Form College

Oldham, England

Oldham, located close to Manchester, has many of the difficult problems of any inner city. An aspect of the mission of the new sixth form college (16-19 years old students) was to address the special needs of this urban context. At the same time, the college promised to be an opportunity for the community to access a state-of-the-art, technology-based education. Industry in Oldham was historically textiles, with declining traditional industries post war. Over the past thirty years, continuing education (or "staying on" for sixth form) was not considered an option for most Oldham students. Students either became manual workers or sought "white collar" jobs in local government.

The goal of the new college was to provide a high quality teaching and learning environment and to improve examination success which was poor. The inability to deliver a quality education in an effective and cost efficient way within many small local sixth form programs was an identified problem. The town of Oldham chose to centralize instruction for the upper secondary student population or the "sixth form" in one building. In the United Kingdom, sixth form is an upper level secondary education that is required for students wishing to go on to university. Traditionally, the classes for the sixth form were held in neighborhood secondary schools. The centralization of all sixth form students into one facility enabled the community to pool resources to create a technology-rich facility. The Oldham Sixth Form College accepted its first class September 1992.

To encourage students to stay in school, the design of the college created a friendly, inviting and welcoming environment in which "young people enjoy their time at school". Reactions to the new facility have been enthusiastic. The school was initially designed for a maximum population of 1000 students. While Sixth Form had historically shown reduced enrollments, the demand to attend the technology-rich Oldham College has been great. The classes entering in 1992 and 1993 have each numbered 600 students, thus putting the enrollment beyond capacity. Plans are currently underway to expand the facility to meet these demands.

New Construction
Occupied: September 1992 (first class)
Architects:
Cruickshank and Seward, Manchester, England
Number of students: designed for 1000, enrolled 600 first year, 600 second year (over capacity)
16-19 age group, optional

PLANNING THE NEW COLLEGE

"It is a community and people have a right to mix and come together as part of their learning process"

Derek Jones Darlington

The college took approximately five years to plan. Derek Jones Darlington, the Project Manager for the Oldham Local Education Authority's Sixth Form reviewed colleges throughout the UK to gather ideas. As this was the first purpose built sixth form college to be built in nearly 20 years, there was little

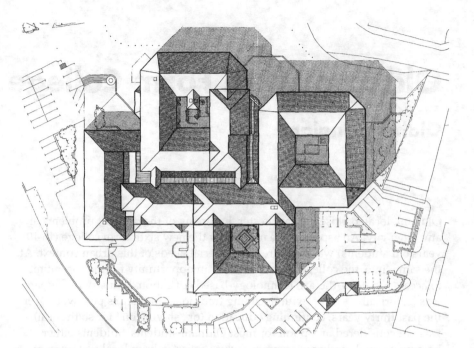

Site Plan

existing good practice to use as a reference for the new building. Planning and design was an interactive process. There was continuous dialogue with the architects and the clients throughout the development of the building.

Design Goals

The first principle of the design was to create a welcoming "building". As well, the building needed to address "how teachers teach and how children learn". Flexibility was seen as key to meeting this goal, to allow teachers to re-configure their environment.

In addition to being a visionary educational center, the community wanted the college to be designed as an urban center. The site chosen for the college was located at an important historic site, the Oldham Royal Infirmary. The difficult site was constricted (with barriers for expansion on nearly all sides), sloping, as well as a demolition site (the Infirmary Building was demolished).

While the planning team had many ideas for the new facility, the project manager cautioned the team not to be "over-reaching". If the ideas for the building and educational program were too far ahead of the community's concept, there was a sense that the program would fail. Finally, the initial brief was provided to the architects in early 1990, with the building being quickly completed in September 1992.

BUILDING DESIGN

You need to feel comfortable. . . . . rather like the English country garden - you enter the garden, but it doesn't reveal all of itself immediately- you are drawn to areas of interest - moving through an archway you are 'taken on' to other parts of the garden - you want to explore it

Derek Jones Darlington

The building is organized with the use of a double height, glazed interior street connecting three courtyard building blocks which house the facility suites. The street is intended to be a place where students wanted to be, where they could "people watch", gather and interact. As the building was envisioned as a public building with an extended day (14 hour), the interior street needed to be inviting to students and to the community.

From this perspective, the building was designed to include a generous allocation of social space and places for individualized learning both centrally (such as the library) and within the faculty suites. The general emphasis on individualized learning made the dispersed study areas the real focus of the building's design.

Natural light and ventilation was an important consideration in the design. The courtyard "buildings" are two to three stories in height. The courtyards bring light and air to the center of each instructional suite. Other facilities located off the street include: a bookstore, information center, conference rooms and a auditorium. In addition the building includes a restaurant (or cafeteria), student lounge and a sports complex.

The interior street provides public space within the school.

Library

The Oldham Sixth Form College library could be considered a model for the "information center" of the future. Unlike the historic model in which students are expected to quietly study and seek books to support their studies, the Oldham College Library is an active place where students can work together in groups, take instruction, access data bases and work on computer workstations. The College's library includes both print and electronic media.

The library and its ancillary spaces are networked, and include computer workstations for student use. The center maintains a large collection of CD ROM disks and holds over 20,000 printed volumes. A connection via modem to the town's central library provides additional access to information. The library is open before and after class hours to allow students to make full use of the building. As the community may also use the library, its entrance is located in close proximity to the building entrance.

The library is designed for many types of learning and research activities including a private study area and two instructional spaces. All three include computer workstations. Students can access the center's holdings from these or from any workstation throughout the college. This zone is built with a raised floor to allow for a flexible arrangement of the workstations.

Faculty Suites

Six academic faculty suites are located by subject area throughout the school. The faculty suite generally includes several classrooms, each seats a maximum of fifteen students, and contains a tutorial area, a study area and a

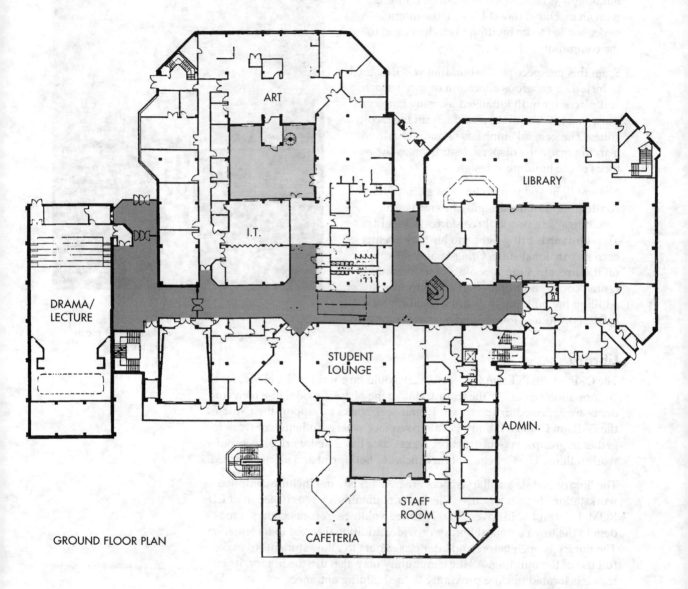

ART

LIBRARY

I.T.

DRAMA/
LECTURE

STUDENT
LOUNGE

ADMIN.

GROUND FLOOR PLAN

STAFF
ROOM

CAFETERIA

resource base (information technology area).
Each suite is designed to meet the specific needs
of each subject and therefore, are not identical to
one another. Partitions separating the classrooms
can be moved to create larger learning spaces and
allowing for the rooms to be "re-configured".

The resource base with networked computer
workstations, and the study area for independent
individual and group study as well as tutorials
are a key aspect of the suite. The resource base
allows for ease of access to technology for learning. This area which is shared between teachers
and students.

Students at work in the
resource base.

Laboratories

The College has a total of ten laboratory spaces, all located on the building's
ground floor. The laboratories are outfitted using the *Lab-Kit* Workstation
System, developed by the Laboratories Investigation Unit of the UK Department for Education. This modular system has been designed to provide the
services needed in a modern science laboratory and yet be flexible. Power,
water and other services are provided by assembling a kit of parts that can
be arranged according to need. All the components of the system can be
disassembled including the service distribution system. Lab benches and
storage units are on wheels and can be easily moved into place.

Language Laboratory

The John F. Kennedy Language Laboratory provides a customized technology-based environment for the study of languages. The lab is equipped with
sixteen hexagonal workstations arranged in groups of four. Each includes a
networked computer with audio and video capabilities. A central console
panel allows an instructor to monitor students' progress. The college receives
all major European television channels using programmers in teaching.

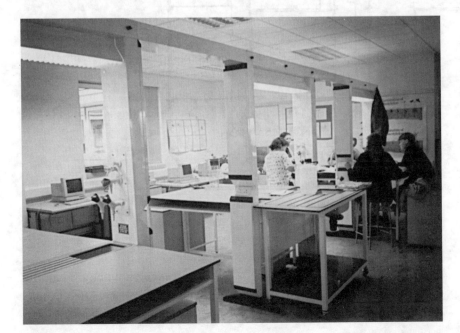

Laboratories are designed
with a modular workstation
system that provides
flexibility in
reorganization.

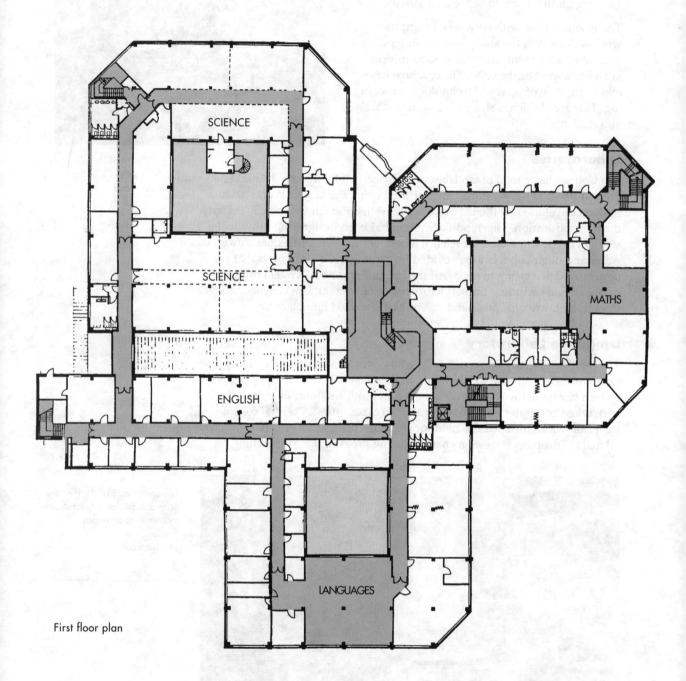

First floor plan

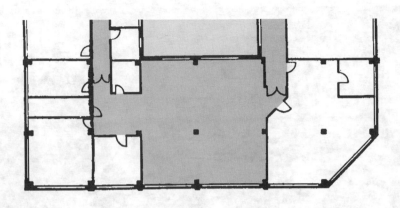

Faculty Suite

TECHNOLOGY

We saw information technology in very philosophical terms at that time, as an enabling function, a credibility giver, something that would meet individual needs; and something that would raise the level of passes by perhaps a grade across the whole college.

Peter Hill, Local Education Authority

As networked computer systems are becoming increasingly common in industry, commerce and education, we feel it is an important part of your IT entitlement to develop confidence in using such systems. . . . we are fortunate in having an advanced "industry standard'" and College-wide network system which links together all of our computers.

Steve Holland, Technology Co-ordinator

Information technology at the college needed to be designed to be readily accessible and uncomplicated. The college's policy was to accomplish three aims:

- make accessible to comprehensive and up-to-date reliable computer technology where the hardware and software systems accurately reflect current commercial practice;

- provide ongoing help in a non-threatening and supportive atmosphere so that everyone has the opportunity to develop and extend their IT capability;

- develop a creative awareness of the applications, strengths, shortcomings, possibilities and implications of IT as technology develops.

Computer workstations are integrated into the labs.

The college emphasizes the use of Apple Macintosh computers but also maintains a large inventory of PC compatible computers (approximately 260, 75% Apple Mac and 25% IBM PC). Every workstation is networked. All students and staff have 'personal storage space' (accounts) on the college's network. Users have access to word processing, spreadsheet, graphics and database software packages. A central technology office manages the college's computer facilities. This office is responsible for the purchase and maintenance of all computer hardware and software.

Information technology is actively used in the language lab.

The network is a multi-platform network. Rather than a more traditional backbone network. Each of the three courtyard buildings is networked independently using a structured cabling architecture in a star topology. Each of these independent networks has its own satellite equipment room. The three buildings are connected to each other by means of a fiber optic cable. Some 600 outlets are provided throughout the college, mostly wall mounted to provide access to the multi-platform computer network.

UPDATE

Steve Holland, Technology Coordinator for the Sixth Form College reports: Our first GCE 'A' level results are excellent, well above national average and would strongly suggest that the college has achieved its prime mission - to increase staying-on rates post 16 and improve examination success. Evening provision begins in September.

Power and network cabling are supplied by simple trunking mounted on the walls.

KEY POINTS

- As the college is designed to prepare students for their future, state of the art information technology is used throughout the school.

- A double-height interior street organizes the plan comprising three courtyard buildings.

- With a shift toward independent learning, study areas are generously provided both centrally and within each faculty area.

- Learning suites include instructional areas, study areas, resource bases (information technology) and tutorials.

- The building has been designed to respond to changes in teaching methods.

- The college uses a building-wide network that allows students access to the library, the central town library, and other data bases.

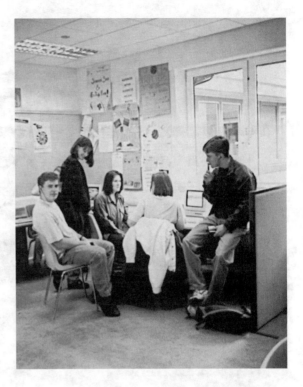

Students gather in a technology resource area.

REFERENCES

Cruickshank and Seward, Architects. Brief on Oldham Sixth Form College.

Steven Holland. Text from presentation at Urban Schools Conference, Lowell, Massachusetts. April 1994.

Koster, Guy. "Synopsis of network installation and infrastructure installed by AEC on behalf of Oldham Metropolitan Borough Council at the Oldham Sixth Form College." AEC, 1994.

Prospectus 1993/94: Choice • Opportunity • Culture. Oldham Education Authority, 1993.

Update 3: Our New College. From Vision to Reality. Oldham Education Authority, Autumn 1992.

ACKNOWLEDGMENTS

This text was developed with assistance from Steven Holland, particularly in the provision of a thoughtful and comprehensive text for his presentation at the Third National Conference on Education and Architecture held at Lowell, Massachusetts in April 1994.

Right: The High Technology High School features a multimedia classroom among its facilities.

Above: The Advanced Technology Center is Brookdale's new teaching facility and telecommunications hub.

Right: Brookdale can downlink virtually any satellite signal with its dishes and receivers.

Brookdale Community College and the High Technology High School

Lincroft, New Jersey, USA

Monmouth County Vocational School District in cooperation with Brookdale Community College has built a "High Technology High School" on the Brookdale campus. This high school complements the college's new Advanced Technology Center (ATeC).

Information networking, distance learning and interactive television have hastened the establishment of relationships between secondary schools and higher education. The situation at Brookdale offers interesting implications for the relationship between secondary schools and higher education.

"The sharing of laboratory training facilities and equipment provides direct linkage between the secondary and college-level programs, reduces duplication of equipment and laboratory space, offers opportunities for exchange by secondary and college [staff], and fosters a continuous curriculum flow from grades 10-14. In addition, the college campus provides a central focal point for potential employers. . . ."

Superintendent, Monmouth County Vocational Schools

The Advanced Technology Center is a teaching facility for the Arts and Communications Division and the Technologies Division, supporting curriculums in telecommunications and engineering technologies. It also serves as the new telecommunications technology hub serving the main campus and off-campus extension sites.

The Advanced Technology Center
Occupied 1990

Total area: 55,000 sq. ft.

Architect: The Architect's Collaborative, Inc., Cambridge, Massachusetts

Cost US $13m

The High Technology High School
Occupied 1991

Total area: 14,000 sq. ft.
Addition area: 11,500 sq. ft.

Architect: Kellenyi Associates, Red Bank, New Jersey

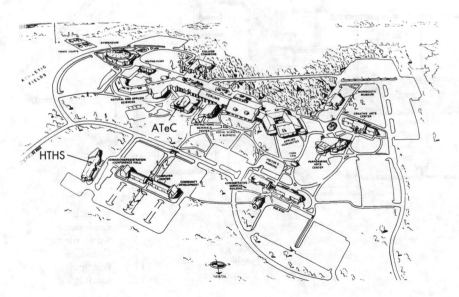

Brookdale Community College Campus Plan

The High Technology High School was constructed on the Brookdale campus through a cooperative agreement between the Monmouth County Vocational School District board of education and the Brookdale College board of trustees. It is designed to include state-of-the-art communications and computer technology and is electronically linked to the ATeC. The high school shares a variety of facilities with the college.

THE HIGH TECHNOLOGY HIGH SCHOOL

This high school offers a specialized curriculum and a limited enrollment of approximately 180 students in grades 10-12 (60 students per year). Beginning in September 1995 the school will include grade nine. The "High Tech High" admits students from each of the 25 other high schools in Monmouth County. The curriculum, called "Engineering Prep," integrates instruction in mathematics and laboratory science with engineering and telecommunications technologies. The high school uses the college's health and fitness facilities. Students also have access to the library and technology courses taught by college faculty in the ATeC. In return, the college and community use the high school facilities in the evening.

Because of the need to share facilities, the high school's course schedule is arranged to coordinate with the college's. Therefore, classes meet an average of three times a week for longer periods of time than in other high school schedules. This also allows students and teachers more uninterrupted time to effectively work on projects. High school students have the option of taking college-level courses after school hours. The school also has instituted a mentoring program with local technology-based firms, such as AT&T, in which students work on research projects in association with that firm.

The school is committed to a multimedia approach in the organization and presentation of information. All students, as well as teachers and administrative staff, use electronic and computer equipment in their work. Every class includes a project component in which each student must present the results of the project to the class in an electronic multimedia format.

High Technology High School Plan prior to addition.

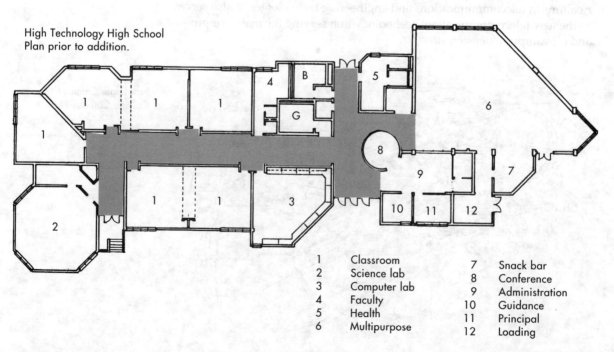

1	Classroom	7	Snack bar
2	Science lab	8	Conference
3	Computer lab	9	Administration
4	Faculty	10	Guidance
5	Health	11	Principal
6	Multipurpose	12	Loading

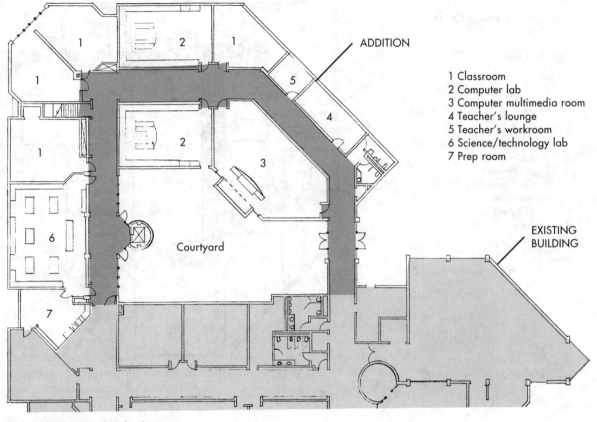

1 Classroom
2 Computer lab
3 Computer multimedia room
4 Teacher's lounge
5 Teacher's workroom
6 Science/technology lab
7 Prep room

High Technology High School
Plan with addition

Technology

Being located on Brookdale's campus, the high school can take advantage of the facilities already in existence and devote its resources to a limited number of technology-intensive facilities, such as two computer centers and a comprehensive science laboratory. The entire high school is networked for voice, data and video to a Novell server located in the administrative office. Located in each room is a communications access plate that integrates a telephone handset, speaker, and data and video jacks. This system also handles the public address/intercom for the school.

In addition, the high school is networked into the campus-wide fiber optic information system, "BluesNet," which allows staff and students to take advantage of all the services available to the college community including teleconferencing, downlinking special programs from satellite broadcasts, and the constant feed of Cable News Network.

The high school administrators have found that, although the relationship between the high school and the college is good, they require more space within their building than they initially planned. The primary problem is an inadequate amount of instruction area. As a result, an addi-

The high school's "head end" is located in the administrative offices.

Case Study Fifteen

Advanced Technology Center

First Level Plan

1 Video production studio
2 Video editing
3 Video control
4 Audio recording studio
5 Audio control
6 Tape storage
7 Video distribution and
   control room
8 Engineering labs
9 Storage

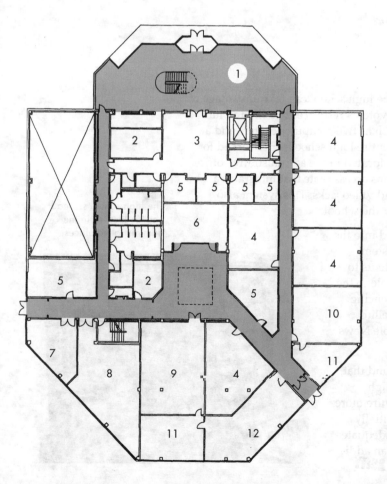

Second Level Plan

1 Lobby
   Reception & exhibit area
2 Conference
3 Administration/reception
4 Classroom
5 Office
6 Student lounge
7 Video training
8 Telephone technology lab
9 Analog lab
10 Microprocessor lab
11 Storage
12 Digital microprocessor lab

tion is planned that will double the existing area. The addition will contain six general classrooms and four specialized labs. These include two computer labs, a computer multimedia room and a science/technology lab.

On June 20, 1994, the first graduating class of 49 students received their diplomas. Eighty percent will pursue higher education degrees in engineering, math, science and technology. All 49 will attend college or university in the fall. Most students will be able to transfer between 16-24 college credits, earned at Brookdale Community College while enrolled at the high school. One student completed both a high school degree simultaneously with an associate's degree in mathematics from Brookdale and will enter university with third year standing (junior).

ADVANCED TECHNOLOGY CENTER (ATeC)

Brookdale Community College's Arts and Communications Division and Technologies Division, located in the ATeC, offers instruction in telecommunications and engineering technologies (including electronics, mechanics, architecture, with manual drafting and computer-assisted drafting). The telecommunications program offers instruction in radio, television and video production; audio recording; and public relations. Brookdale's recording, production and broadcasting facilities offer students the opportunity to acquire practical experience in preparing for employment within the industry. The ATeC also offers worker training, skills development and teacher training courses.

Brookdale runs an extensive "telecourse" program. Students who are unable to attend classes on-campus, or at prescribed times, may view recorded courses either at the campus or at home. Classes are also broadcast by local cable TV services. The telecourses are produced at the ATeC. During the winter 1993 semester, Brookdale ran 16 telecourses in 11 subject areas via cable, and broadcast six radio courses.

BUILDING DESIGN

The ATeC is a three-story structure which houses two distinct groups. The first and second levels are used by the telecommunications and engineering technologies divisions. The third floor is occupied by the Business Training and Development Center and the Center for Human and Industrial Productivity. Both centers serve the business community by offering seminars, conferences and customized courses.

The telecommunications technologies area includes a radio station suite, a media production center and professional quality video and audio production facilities. The media production center provides audio and video instruction facilities which are utilized by students on an informal basis. These facilities are used by the teachers and students in conjunction with technical staff to produce a variety of products such as taped classes for the distance learning program and a weekly news magazine called *Brookdale Today*, which is produced by students and transmitted on the campus network.

The video production facilities include a 2,000 square foot, three-camera television studio and control room. A separate heating, ventilation and air conditioning system is provided to control excessive heat generated by studio lighting. The sensitivity of the audio recording done in the studio demands that the HVAC system produce no audible mechanical noise.

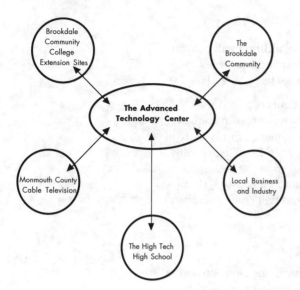

A professional quality audio studio allows for performances to be recorded and produced. This facility has an adjacent production/control room with recording and mixing equipment. It is supported by several electronic music studios and recording labs.

These facilities are staffed by technical staff and teachers who supervise students in the use of the facilities and equipment. The smaller audio and video production studios are available for students to spend more time working without direct supervision. This allows students to improve their skills in studio production, the use of portable video, and editing.

Telecommunications Network

The ATeC functions as the campus telecommunications hub. The network operates on a fiber optic backbone that supports an integrated voice, video, data network, called "BluesNet." In addition to being networked to every classroom, BluesNet also links the 36 computing labs on campus, Brookdale's extension sites in Asbury Park and Bayshore, and the High Technology High School.

BluesNet carries an eight-channel cable television system as well as data and voice signals. One cable channel is dedicated to the campus bulletin board, another channel is dedicated to Cable News Network, and the remaining channels are programmed as required. The local telephone utility provides Brookdale with a fiber optic service for the campus phone system as well as for data and video. This provides Brookdale with a direct connection to the local cable companies, which permits cooperative arrangements between the college and the cable companies for distance learning programs and other possible ventures.

The ATeC features a professional quality television studio and video control room.

The ATeC also houses the video distribution and control room, or "head end," for the BluesNet and three satellite receivers. The control system uses a touch screen router which allows network connections to be configured very simply at a computer workstation. The three satellite receivers, one KU band and two C band, can downlink virtually any signal. When an uplink is required, time can be rented from the Comcast Corporation nearby.

Brookdale has four satellite dishes located at ground level adjacent to the ATeC. The primary concerns that were considered in locating the dishes were the assurance of a clear line of sight between each dish and the target satellite and the ability to run conduit for cabling to the ATeC. In addition, there was some initial concern about the possibility of tampering since the dishes are located in an open accessible area. In the two and one-half years that the dishes have been in place, no problems of this nature have been experienced.

The ATeC has a system of open metal cable trays designed to facilitate cable management. Each tray is divided into three sections to further rationalize the organization of the cabling and separate power from data and video cabling.

KEY POINTS

The High Technology High School

- Cooperative arrangement allowed the construction of a new high school on Brookdale's campus.

- High school and college share facilities.

- Specialized science and math high school offers "engineering prep" curriculum and a limited enrollment.

- All students, faculty and staff use computer equipment in their work in a commitment to a multimedia approach to education.

The Advanced Technology Center

- The ATeC is a teaching facility for telecommunications and engineering technology that serves as a telecommunications hub for the college.

- An integrated voice, video and data network, "BluesNet," links classrooms, offices, computer labs and extension sites in Asbury Park and Bayshore.

- The ATeC operates three satellite receivers and an eight-channel cable television system.

- The ATeC features a 2,000 sq ft television studio and a professional quality audio recording studio.

The entrance to one of the
Lindholmen buildings.

An aerial view of the
Hisingen port area.

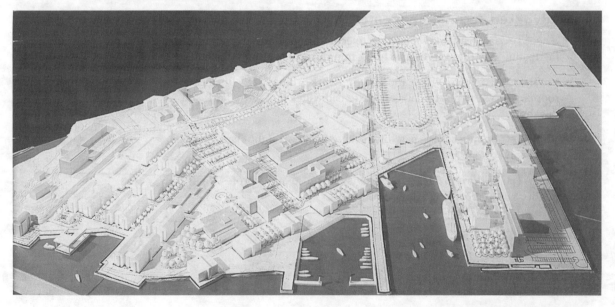

View of the Linholmen site
model.

Case Study Sixteen

Lindholmen Centre for Knowledge

Gothenburg, Sweden

The Centre for Knowledge at Lindholmen is an example of a large scale response to changes in education, information technology and the economy. In the case of Gothenberg, Sweden, one of the key changes in the late 1970s and 1980s was from labor intensive manufacturing and shipbuilding industries to computer-aided manufacturing and other industries. In creating a new working and learning environment from a redundant industrial site, the city's goal was to develop a new education and research community which would also include residential buildings safely mixed with clean industry.

Architect: White Architect
Cost: SKr 500 000 000
Area: 100,000 sq. meters

The "Centre for Knowledge" comprises a complex of new and refurbished facilities within a larger regeneration zone. The Centre offers education for upper secondary level students, adults, university students and government sponsored retraining programs for unemployed workers and those whose jobs are deemed at risk due to technological change. It also includes a research and development component involved in information and technology transfer. The Centre supports a strong connection between industry, education and research with an emphasis on the importance of education in a technology-based economy and the need for lifelong learning.

History of the Lindholmen Development

The Lindholmen development is one part of the master plan to revitalize the inner harbor of an area called Hisingen. Five shipyards in this area provided employment and economic stability for the Gothenburg region until the mid 1970s. When they closed, more than 15,000 workers needed to be retrained for other employment. Lindholmen was one of the shipyards which closed in 1975-76. The shipyards were large industrial areas which required consideration for redevelopment and reuse. The total area for redevelopment is 250 hectares. The Lindholmen area is nearly 60 hectares, half of which is allocated for the Centre for Knowledge.

Entrance to Lindholmen from the water-bus.

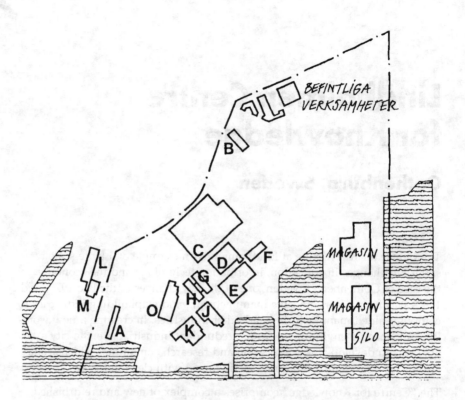

Site plan of the
Lindholmen complex
(shaded area is the Gota
River)

In 1987, a concept emerged to revitalize this area, including education, offices and residences. The plan to create the Centre for Knowledge at Lindholmen was developed employing the idea that lifelong learning was a necessary element in revitalizing the economy and preparing the population for industry shifts and changes in employment, particularly with increased use of information technology. The first stage of development began in 1990 with a detailed plan being released in June 1989 for three areas: Erikberg, Sannegarden and Lindholmen. "The Centre for Knowledge was a collaborative effort between the City of Gothenburg (through the city's Board of Education and the owner, Lindholmen, which is a city owned company) and the Swedish state (through the National Vocational Training Scheme and Chalmers University of Technology)."

Centre for Knowledge

The Centre combines three complimentary activities: learning, research and development, and technology-based production. The Centre provides educational programs for four high schools, adult education, worker retraining and graduate and undergraduate university students. Educational programs will be offered for the elderly, in keeping with the philosophy of promoting lifelong learning.

The educational setting was designed to bring together students from different sectors. Having a mix of students within the same environment was intended to promote exchange between students. Students can also benefit from cross-sector course work. Information technology, particularly networked computer workstations provide a flexible learning environment which can be used for many different applications and educational purposes. The same facility and computer equipment can be used to teach university students, high school students or to retrain workers.

Within this philosophy, the shipyard facilities were renovated to provide an educational environment that is attractive, meets the needs of specific vocational programs (for example, the Culinary Arts School), and creates an open environment that encourages students to collaborate with one another. To reinforce the importance of learning and the fact that learning is life long, the founders thought the mix of students was very important. School age students should be able to interact with adult learners as well as workers all learn within a shared educational environment.

Computer workstation at Lindholmen.

The setting includes three adult schools: (1) a Basic School (basic skills and literacy teaching for adult immigrants + Junior High School, (2) Upper Secondary School (high school equivalent), and (3) a Production Technology Center (technical curriculum such as robotics, computer-aided controls, drafting and manufacturing). These three schools share services and resources including staff, facilities, administration, and financing.

New Technology

One of the key motivations for the Centre for Knowledge was an understanding that as Gothenburg's economic base was changing, the requirements for work were changing as well. An important aspect of this shift was the role of information technology in the workplace. Students require an educational program which would reinforce the use of new information technology in design and development as well as in manufacturing.

Industry participated in the development of educational programs that are relevant to the workplace. Industry representatives indicated that there was a gap between the requirements for employment and educational programs. One goal was to make the educational program more closely connected with these requirements and in the process, address larger issues regarding economic development. For example, Volvo Data AB developed a relationship with the Centre allowing students to use the company's computer-

Courtyard and entrance at the Centre.

Right and opposite page: The master plan for Lindholmen and the entire Hisingen area required the preservation of the character of the traditional buildings of the area and the integration of housing with other uses in the former industrial area.

aided design software on their main frame computer via a network. In this way, students could learn directly on the software which is currently being used in the industry. This relationship also equipped the Centre to be able to retrain Volvo employees as required. Other industry-based educational programs include robotics and computer-aided manufacturing.

Bringing diverse educational sectors together within a learning environment and readdressing the nature of work through technology-based learning held much promise for redefining the industrial process in general. The research component of the Centre further addresses many of these issues including work organization, ergonomics, production processes and technology, as well as work environment concerns.

BUILDING DESIGN

The key goals for the design of the Centre included: (1) to reuse existing buildings, conserving the historic character of the ship building site, (2) to integrate educational sectors in a shared learning environment, and (3) to provide a technology-rich educational setting. The physical environment was to incorporate the ideas and visions of the Centre, offering an alternative learning environment as part of a "campus infrastructure" as a new model for a city.

These renovated industrial buildings, offer a comfortable and interesting learning environment, demonstrating that the technology-rich learning environment does not require new construction.

Some features of the buildings allowed for open atriums that brought natural light into the educational setting. In keeping with the concept of providing for exchange between students, small study areas and meeting areas are located within the corridors. Teachers offices and workrooms are intended to promote teacher interaction. Within the computer aided manufacturing area, computer labs are located alongside the industry floor for instruction and

design development, furthering the conceptual connection between technology application and industry. As the Centre is also involved with research and development in ergonomics, some attention has been given to assure that the computer workstations are designed to be ergonomically correct.

Key Points

- Lindholmen Centre for Knowldege is a mixed use development within a larger zone of regeneration that includes education, housing and industry.

- The master plan calls for the reuse of existing buildings and the conservation of the historic character of the area.

- The centre is designed to support lifelong learning.

- It is a technology-rich learning environment that brings together diverse educational sectors: secondary school students, university students, adult learners, and retraining workers.

- The research and development component engages in information and technology transfer.

Above right: The atrium links the five main blocks of the campus and provides a sun-lit meeting place.

Above: Power and network connections are supplied via the structural column in this open work area.

Right: The entrance of Tea Tree Gully Campus.

Tea Tree Gully Campus of Torrens Valley Institute of Tafe
Adelaide, Australia

Tea Tree Gully, Campus of TAFE of the Torrens Valley Institute has developed a facility which attempts to create a supportive environment for individualized learning via technology. Tea Tree Gully Campus is the first institution of higher learning in Australia that is designed for Open Learning or a student-centered approach to learning. The facility operates as a collection of five main building blocks, each composed of "educational suites" devoted to a number of related subject areas. Subject matter is primarily vocational, focusing on industries that are currently confronting or predicted to experience personnel shortages. Education at the campus is via two modes. Most academic and business related coursework is self-directed using computers. Additional vocational training occurs in settings that simulate work environments.

TEACHING AND LEARNING

The Open Learning pedagogy at Tea Tree Gully Campus is driven by an approach to curriculum that is based on proficiency rather than "time served". Success under the Competency Based Training (CBT) system is seen as the ability to demonstrate competencies, knowledge and skills. Learning is no longer tied to a specific location, teaching method or to the amount of time spent in class. Rather, the system lends itself to self-directed learning and to the mastery of skills. Competency Based Training has become part of a national training reform agenda. Beginning in 1993/1994, every curriculum document in Australia is to be written using the competency based format.[1]

Competency Based Training implies "flexibility" in course arrangements and a more learner centered approach to study. The campus maintains an "Open Entry/Open Exit" policy which allows students to begin courses at their own choosing. Students learn at their own pace, guiding themselves through course materials. They determine when to pursue their studies and the amount of time and effort that they can devote. Students earn credit for previous learning and experience whether or not it was gained in a classroom. Students begin their studies at an appropriate level by completing a series of diagnostic or "challenge" tests.

The curriculum at Tea Tree Gully College provides a vocational education intended to give students skills that they can bring to the work environment. Educational programs have been designed to address "areas of identified skills shortage". Graduates of these programs have the skills needed for employment in information and service industries. Areas of study include: computing and information systems, business and commercial studies, electronics and information technology, hospitality and community services.[2]

New Construction
Higher Education (further education)
Architect: Andrew Gehling of SACON (So. Australian Dept. of Housing and Construction)
Occupied: Officially opened February 1992
Stage I: November 1991
Stage II: March 1992
Capacity:
equivalent to 1800 full-time students
Will reach full capacity 1994
Cost: A$29.9 million

Each Learning Assistance Center serves as a mini-library for its educational suite.

In order to support this Open Learning environment, emphasis has been placed creating teams of professions to provide support for students. Each team consists of advanced skill lecturers, lecturers and lecturer's assistants, technicians and support staff. The team approach allows educators to develop specific skills that benefit the entire team and their students. The concept of participation and self-direction has been applied to the educational teams. The teams are self-managing. They negotiate their own performance agreement with management.[3]

BUILDING DESIGN

The newly constructed facility is located on a 5.5 hectare site in a suburb of Adelaide in South Australia. The site was previously undeveloped or a "greenfield site". The college is well connected to the local mass transit system. The main entrance to the facility is directly opposite the O-Bahn Rapid Transit System Interchange.

Computer workstaions are grouped around a "power pole" that supplies power and network cabling.

Tea Tree Gully College is composed of five main, two-story blocks linked by a glazed atrium and concourse. The buildings were constructed in two stages. First, three of the main blocks and the lecture theatre. These include: (1) the library, (2) the amenities block and (3) the learning block. The final two blocks, (4) the workshop block and (5) the multipurpose hall, were completed during the second stage of the project. The internal atrium and concourse, together with an external pedestrian street, serve as an organizing element for the entire complex. The amenities block, the "learning block" and the workshop block each house one or more educational suites.

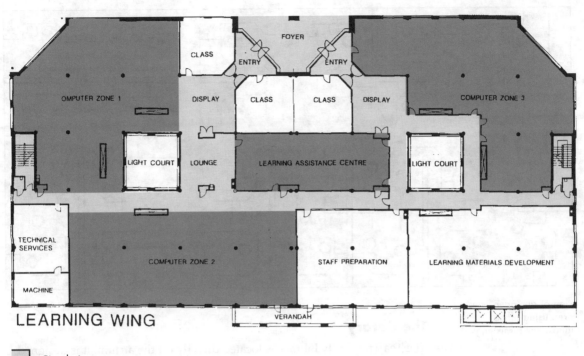

LEARNING WING

Circulation

Computer Zones

Educational Suites

Several features are common to each educational suite: the entry and display areas, the independent study area(s), a student lounge, the "Learning Assistance Center" and the staff preparation area. The entry and display areas give each suite a separate identity and each has its own entrance from the atrium. The display area provides a transition space between the entry and the rest of the suite and can be used to display student work. The independent study area is designed for self directed learning using computers. The area supports individual project work and work done by groups. The student lounge is adjacent to the independent study area. As instruction is self-directed, the lounge provides a place "to take a break" from the computer. It provides a space for students to gather and discuss their work.

A learning assistance center (LAC) is located at the core of each educational suite. Each functions as a mini-library or resource center. It houses materials needed for current course offerings as well as additional support materials to the subject area. Materials may be printed or in video or audio form.

At Tea Tree Gully, educational quality relies on the quality of the course material. In effect, curriculum development plays a significant role in the success of the college. The staff preparation areas enable educational teams to develop course materials as well as prepare for lessons.

Furniture has been specially designed for the independent study areas and learning assistance centers. The office landscape furnishings create effective work areas suitable for an individual or a group. The casework accommodates student workstations and a means of networking. The casework allows for the efficient use of space since it can be utilized in the interior of the room as well as placed along the perimeter.

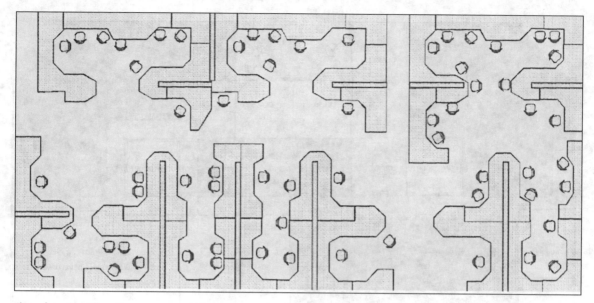

Plan of an "open" study area using office landscape furnishings.

The Library

The Tea Tree Gully Library is located directly off the atrium. It is designed to meet student needs as well as those of the entire community as it is operated jointly by the institute and the City of Tea Tree Gully. In addition to the main collection, it has a large children's collection and a children's activity area. Meeting rooms are designated for community and student use.

The Amenities Block

The amenities block is devoted to hospitality education. Tea Tree Gully offers courses in cookery and food service. Learning spaces include: the learning assistance center, a classroom, the training kitchen, the restaurant, lounge and bar. The amenities block also houses the social gathering space for the campus: the student center, the cafeteria, and student and staff lounges. The campus' main offices are located on the upper level.

The Learning Block

The lower level of the learning block contains the areas devoted to health and beauty studies and to community services. Entrances at either end of the suite provide direct access to each area. The suite is designed to provide a vocational and academic learning environment. The learning assistance center is at the core. There are several specialized vocational spaces such as salons, a beauty therapy lab, a personal care lab and a crèche, or nursery. Classrooms and seminar spaces are also provided.

Business and commercial studies and computing and information systems are located on the upper level. The suite consists primarily of the learning assistance center and three computer zones. The computer zones are mainly used for self-directed learning. The suite also includes substantial staff preparation and learning materials development areas.

Students at work in an independant study area.

TECHNOLOGY

While most educational programs are delivered through the use of computer assisted learning, other technologies are also in use. These include: interactive video and compact discs, video and teleconferencing, and television provided via satellite or fiber-optic cabling. All of these technologies are also required for the development of new learning materials.

Perhaps the most important use of technology at the school is in maintaining student records. The campus has facilities for the 1800 full-time equivalent students. Open enrollment and the fact that most students are enrolled on a part-time basis has led the campus to rely upon a sophisticated computer system to track students through their coursework.[4]

Office-type landscape furniture is used to create "open" work areas where computers are available for use.

KEY POINTS

- The facility is composed of five main two-story blocks linked by a glazed internal atrium and concourse.

- The college uses a Competency Based Training (CBT) approach to education that values competency, knowledge and skills.

- CBT implies flexibility in delivering materials to students and responsibility on the part of students. Tea Tree Gully College stresses these qualities by incorporating recognition of prior learning, open entry/open exit and self-paced learning.

- Educational teams design, teach and administer all of the college's academic and vocational programs.

- A Learning Assistance Center (LAC) is at the core of each educational suite, functioning as a mini-library or resource center.

- Each suite includes a staff preparation area. This area provides a setting for curriculum development.

- Other vocational training occurs in simulated work environments.

REFERENCES

[1] Tony Ryan "Greenfield, Site to Open Learning," *Adult Education News: Newsletter of the Australian Association of Adult and Community Education* , Australian Post: Publication no. NBH 0921, July 1992, p.14.

[2] "Tea Tree Gully College of TAFE: A College for the 21st Century." Brief Overview. Brochure from Tea Tree Gully.

[3] Michael Sachsse. "Open Learning: Its Implication for Students and Teachers." Post Compulsory Education 93 Directions Conference. Perth, Australia, November, 21-23, 1993, p.4.

[4] Sachsse, p.3.

The entrance to the library is on the mid-level via a bridge over the main campus walkway.

Tilburg University Library

Tilburg, The Netherlands

"Science, which needs to keep pace with the developments in society, and which would preferably have to be a few steps ahead, deserves a modern infrastructure."

Board of Governors, Tilburg University, 1985[1]

The new library at Tilburg University was designed and constructed to support the education and research needs of teachers and students through automation and computerization. Given this directive, the goal was to build a new library which would be flexible enough to adapt to changing educational and research needs, accommodate a fiber optic network with distribution to integrated workstations, and support a range of possible arrangements. The library planners worked closely with the staff of the university computing center and Digital Equipment Corporation, to design an electronic information resource network which would enhance the development and dissemination of scientific knowledge. This network is designed as a key element of the university library's vision of availability of powerful computer workstations to access and marshal an array of information resources. Their goal is to provide:

New Construction
Occupied: 1992
Total area: 9 460 m2
Construction: US$14.8 million
Computer equipment:
US$6.8 million
FDDI Network: US$686 000
Architect: Martien Jansen
OD 205, Eindhoven
The Netherlands

- ease of access to local and remote resources;

- computers and work space for research and study;

- integrated workstations for all aspects of information handling;

- accessibility to these resources from home;

- easy to use on-campus as well as long-distance network communication.

Through automation and computerization, traditional administrative tasks such as lending and tracking were eliminated leaving more time for staff to help students and academics. Staff also have more time to test new software, develop easier and faster methods of accessing long-distance information and communications, maintain and update existing data bases and include new data bases, on the network. These services are performed in an effort to accommodate changing research needs.

BUILDING DESIGN

The library is centrally located on the campus at the intersection of the two main pedestrian walkways. The location was chosen to symbolize the central place which knowledge holds in the life of the university, and more practically, so that the library is easily accessible to all campus faculties. The main entrance is located at the middle level of the three-story structure

The separation between
the structure and the
exterior wall allows for
ease of networking
along the perimeter.

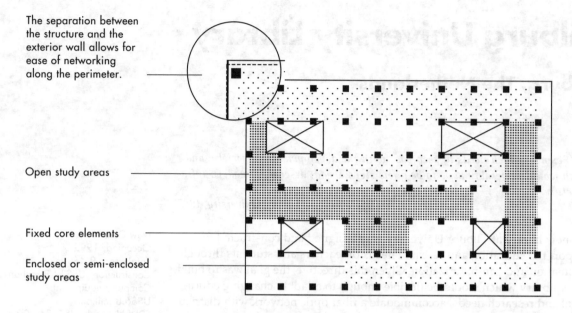

Open study areas

Fixed core elements

Enclosed or semi-enclosed
study areas

Diagram: Mid-Level Plan

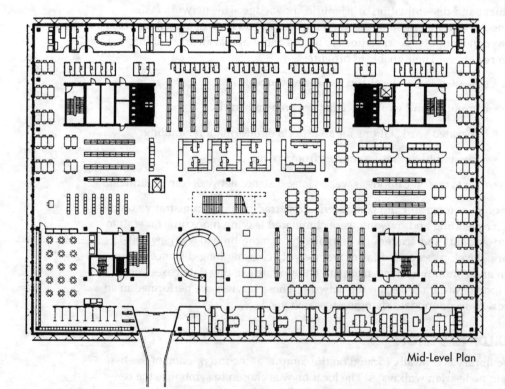

Mid-Level Plan

reached by a bridge. The two upper floors have semi-open plans and contain the main traffic and use areas. The ground floor is used as storage. They are connected by a wide central staircase. A skylight above the staircase brings daylight into the center of the building. On the exterior, the ground floor is partially hidden by earth berms.

The use of a columnar structure eliminates the need for structural or load-bearing walls and facilitates flexibility. A reinforced concrete frame was chosen for both structural and aesthetic reasons.

The pre-stressed concrete floor slabs were chosen for their load-bearing capacity. The exterior is clad in concrete panels with regularly spaced windows with metal shading devices. The concrete structural elements are exposed throughout the building to clearly distinguish these permanent members from the less permanent finish elements. This structure was chosen as providing the most flexibility in terms of changing configurations in response to future needs and changes in technology.

Lighting

One important feature is the control of natural daylight. While a view to the outside is generally preferred, ultraviolet radiation from daylight can speed the decay of printed materials and can induce eye strain if monitors are viewed against a bright background. The designers used exterior metal louvers to filter the strong sunlight in combination with good interior lighting. The louvers maintained the view while reducing the contrast between the outside and inside luminous environments. The interior was designed to provide a general uniform lighting level so that when layout changes are made, good lighting is maintained. Earth berms created against the exterior walls on the ground level help to protect the permanent storage areas by reducing cooling loads. Small windows placed above the berms provide views to the outside without allowing harmful radiation into the storage areas.

Campus Plan

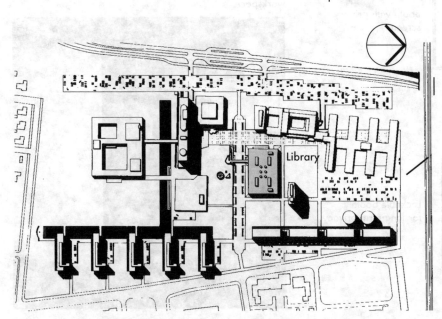

Modular casework was designed to meet the requirements of specific uses.

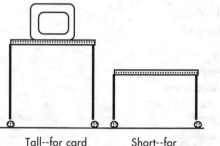

Tall--for card catalogue reference while standing

Short--for desk work

The multifunctional use of the modern University Library as a technological knowledge centre requires a design with the option of putting together various combinations.

Board of Governors, Tilburg University

The building incorporates a variety of study areas for individuals and small groups. These are designed to provide different degrees of privacy depending upon the nature of the work or research done. These areas are located around the building's perimeter, providing views to the outside. They include individual study cubicles, tables in clusters of two to four, small group meeting rooms, conference rooms and seminar rooms. Many of the areas include networked computer workstations. Visiting faculty or students conducting long-term research can reserve a "study cabin." These are free standing, four-sided, screened-in work areas with a personal computer and surface space for books, paper and supplies, and are lockable. There are also two glass-enclosed audio labs providing work space that is acoustically separated from outside noise while still visually connected to the library.

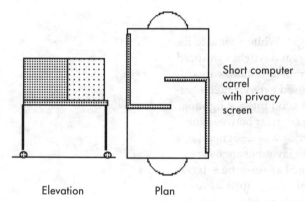

Elevation

Plan

Short computer carrel with privacy screen

Booth with privacy screen

Plan

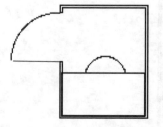

Lockable booth for long-term privacy

Plan

Below: "Study cabins" provide private workspace.

Left: Workstations can be added as needed with the use of "energy pillars" and modular furnishings.

INFORMATION TECHNOLOGY

The library's connection to the campus fiber optic network provides for high-speed data transmission. The campus backbone is configured as a ring with individual spokes to each department. This configuration provides each department with access to the library's internal Ethernet. The campus network has more than 2,500 connecting points installed, with 2,000 computers currently on-line, leaving capacity for future growth.

Tilburg University Library is working in cooperation with the University of Barcelona in Spain, the University of Patras in Greece, Digital Equipment Corporation and Synar Corporation in The Netherlands on the Telephassa Project. This collaboration has resulted in the development of interactive multimedia products designed for library use. The Tilburg Library and De Montfort University in England, IBM UK, and The Victoria and Albert Museum (London) are engaged in a project to develop colored image bands in a European Community sponsored project.

These activities require the physical design to provide ease of access to information and long-distance communication. The University Library is not only a source of information but also a meeting place. It must be possible to collect influences from outside.

Martien Jansen, Architect

"Lendomat"

Lending and up-to-the-minute listing of holdings are computerized. This frees up time for the staff and eliminates the need for a collections desk. Each student, faculty member and university employee carries an electronic identification and account card known as the "KUB card." Each card has a computer chip that can be read by electronic devices. This card enables patrons to check out and return books themselves. If permission is denied, the electronic gates located at the exit detect unauthorized lending.

To return books, borrowers go to another Lendomat, insert their KUB card and re-scan each book code. If the information is acceptable, books are elec-

Above: Students use the Lendomat to checkout and return books.

tronically recorded as "present" and taken away by a conveyor belt. If the book is returned late, the information is recorded on the borrower's KUB card, and the amount owed is automatically deducted from the card. The KUB card will soon be usable with photocopiers and vending machines.

Computer Workstations

Four hundred fifty computer workstations are located throughout the library to access networks, databases, and for communication. Each station is connected to the fiber optic network. Word processing, database management, spread sheets and software are available at each workstation. More services are available through connections to department networks through the university fileserver which maintains specialized software and links to external networks which open the doors to global communication and collaboration. Access to these additional services is granted according to the users' research needs.

HVAC, Networking and Structure

With the introduction of 450 or more workstations, climate control is necessary to sustain both human comfort and the safe operation of computers. An interstitial space of 1.5 meters (4.9 feet) between the ceiling and floor of the upper levels houses the HVAC and cabling distribution equipment. "Energy pillars" are used as conduits

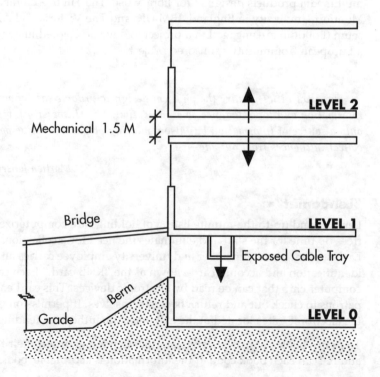

Partial Section Diagram

to bring power and cables from the ceiling to workstation clusters. Energy pillars can quickly be relocated to access electric power and information networks in the ceiling. The separation between the structure and the exterior wall allows for ease of networking along the perimeter.

The furniture is an integral part of the cable and power distribution system. Most of the furniture is modular with special systems developed for workstations and study cabins. Tables are designed with tabletop openings for bringing cables through to a thin horizontal tray which carries the cables to an "energy pillar" or wall-mounted chase. L-shaped screens at each station provide a degree of individual privacy and space efficiency without completely blocking the light as well as the view of others.

Below: On-line catalogue terminals are placed at tall stations for quick reference and seated stations for longer-term use.

KEY POINTS

- The FDDI Network serves as a backbone, while the library is wired with Ethernet. The network will be appended in the next years.

- Modular furniture system is a key element in network distribution system.

- A variety of study areas are offered.

- HVAC and cable management systems integrated.

- Structure designed for flexibility in relation to changes in technology.

REFERENCES

- *Tilburg University. The University Library of the Future Today.* Tilburg: Tilburg University Press, 1992

145

Above: Implementation of ITG typically requires two instructional spaces dedicated to technology instruction. Pictured is a computer workshop.

Right: In the technology lab, students write simple programs to control machines such as this one.

Landesbildstelle

Berlin, Germany

The Landesbildstelle plays a central role in a program designed to provide Berlin's teachers with the training necessary to implement and carry out a technology-based curriculum. This program recognizes that teachers and their schools need an effective support mechanism at both the technology level (hardware and software) and the skill level (teacher training). The Landesbildstelle provides technology training for the city's teachers as well as serving as a central clearinghouse to supply and service computer equipment for the city's schools.

The Berlin Landesbildstelle, which can be described as a "media center", is a central information and education resource. The Landesbildstelle has worked in cooperation with the Berlin Senatsschulverwaltung (the public education governing body, roughly equivalent to a board of education) and the Berlin Institute for Lehrerfortbildung BIL (teacher's training center) to integrate a new "technology" curriculum into the larger curriculum. This "Informationstechnische Grundbildung" (ITG) is designed to teach basic competencies in the use of information technology. ITG has been integrated as part of another relatively new subject called "Arbeitslehre," or workplace training.

Arbeitslehre and ITG

Two main areas were identified as being most directly affected by changing information technologies: the design and production of industrially produced commodities, and administration and bookkeeping. In comprehensive schools and the Hauptschule, students are taught ITG as part of the Arbeitslehre in the eighth grade. At the secondary level, the Realschule and Gymnasium offer a special ITG subject area.

The basic components of ITG are:

- introduction to computer devices and comprehension of computer technology,
- the handling of computers and peripheral equipment,
- problems of protecting personal data,
- the development of electronic data processing,
- application and control of technology,
- problem solving using algorithms,
- social and economic consequences of the widespread use of microelectronics,
- the opportunities and risks of using information technology and developing a sensible relation to them,
- the ability to judge personal experiences related to computer technology.

A hands-on technology lab is part of a pair of instruction spaces for ITG.

After finishing the eighth grade, students choose either of two areas they wish to study further. Students who are interested in technical applications of computer technology continue using CNC machines, CAD systems and educational interfaces to control machinery through computers. Students who are interested in administration can study word processing, data bases and other business applications.

INSTRUCTIONAL FACILITIES

The instruction of ITG takes place in a suite of two rooms, although not all schools are able to provide two rooms yet. The first is a computer workshop where students are introduced to the basics of computer use and work on elements of programming and program applications. The second is the hands-on technology lab. This lab is equipped with workbenches, electrical components and some machinery. In this room students apply the programs they write in the workshop to control machinery and mechanical models, which they usually also make. Students investigate aspects of electronic technology in detail to understand the principles of how computers operate. Typically, students first spend time in the computer workshop learning about programming and then move to the hands-on lab to apply their work accomplished in the first room.

TEACHER TRAINING

The Landesbildstelle is an important resource in Berlin's effort to implement a technology curriculum. Among the problems associated with this effort is the fact that many teachers are not trained in the use of computer technologies for instruction. Teachers' training is organized in cooperation with the BIL. Teachers attend a half-year course in which they become familiar with the educational technology used in teaching ITG. Teachers choose an area of specialization, either technical or administrative applications.

The Landesbildstelle supplies the city's schools with educational materials, software, and audiovisual materials such as slides and videos, and serves as a technical resource for the schools.

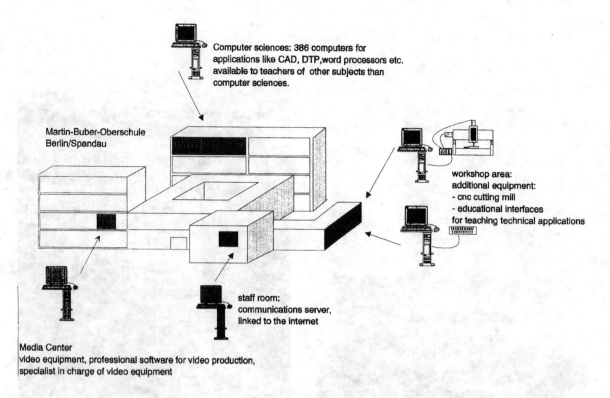

Computer sciences: 386 computers for applications like CAD, DTP,word processors etc. available to teachers of other subjects than computer sciences.

Martin-Buber-Oberschule Berlin/Spandau

workshop area:
additional equipment:
- cnc cutting mill
- educational interfaces
for teaching technical applications

staff room:
communications server,
linked to the internet

Media Center
video equipment, professional software for video production,
specialist in charge of video equipment

Technical support and teacher training are essential aspects of the success of a technology curriculum. Individual teachers and schools do not have the time or resources to organize technical aspects of such a program. It is useful, therefore, to have an entity such as the Landesbildstelle for organization and support.

KEY POINTS

- The Landesbildstelle is a central resource to support the implementation of a comprehensive technology component within the Berlin school's curriculum.

- It provides Berlin's teachers with training necessary to implement the technology-based curriculum and specialized teacher training facilities.

- It functions as a central distribution point for the purchase and repair of computer equipment and software.

- It provides technical support for the city schools carrying out the technology curriculum.

Acknowledgment

Diagram provided by Joachim Hoeret.

Above right: TIC is
located in a complex of
turn-of-the-century former
school buildings.

Above: The research
center develops
educational software and
multimedia applications
for use in the classroom.

Right: The Open
Computer Workshop is a
drop-in center where the
public can use
information technology
and receive informal
assistance from the staff.

TIC – Technology Information Center

Copenhagen, Denmark

TIC was established in 1984 as a cooperative venture by two departments of the city administration – the education authority and the labor department. The initial focus of the center's operation was to provide support for the use of information technology in the city schools and worker training. Within the first year of operation, TIC's scope of work rapidly expanded to include programs and services for the unemployed, business and industry, municipal employees, and the general public. Courses in basic computing are available for the unemployed. Teachers receive training in how to use computers in teaching, and municipal employees are taught how to use computers more efficiently in their work. TIC's Open Computer Workshop and information technology library are open to the general public. Other support facilities include instructional classrooms, studios and other work spaces, and staff offices.

Training and Services

An important aspect of the work of TIC is to provide training to unemployed young people. TIC offers work as an "assistant" for a period seven months. During this time assistants work with the full-time staff in the operation of the center including management and distribution of resources and teaching others in the use of information technology resources. In this way, they learn by doing and teaching. In the process they acquire transferable skills for further employment. Approximately 150 people are employed at the center for 20 to 37 hours a week. Those who finish TIC's work program have a 70-80 per cent rate of success in finding subsequent employment. TIC also conducts technology training courses for city employees and for employees in the private sector.

One of TIC's main services is providing support programs for school teachers. Teachers are trained in the use of computer technology for instruction at the center. Trainers also visit schools to hold sessions and work in support of the technology programs in the schools. TIC supplies computer equipment to the city's schools acting as a purchasing and distribution center. The staff provides technical advice as well as equipment maintenance and repair services.

Another important service is software development. TIC staff have developed educational software and multimedia applications for use at the center and by the teachers in the schools. TIC translates instruction manuals into Danish for general use.

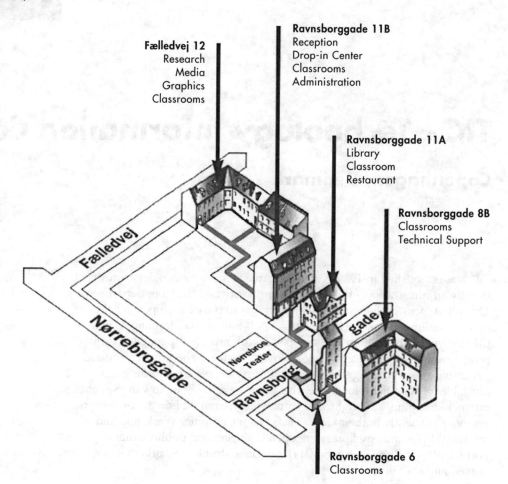

Fælledvej 12
Research
Media
Graphics
Classrooms

Ravnsborggade 11B
Reception
Drop-in Center
Classrooms
Administration

Ravnsborggade 11A
Library
Classroom
Restaurant

Ravnsborggade 8B
Classrooms
Technical Support

Ravnsborggade 6
Classrooms

Building Design

TIC is located in a complex of turn-of-the-century buildings, including two that were formerly used as school buildings, which have been renovated and adapted for use by TIC.

The center houses studios and workrooms for the preparation of educational software and computer and audio-visual equipment for distribution to the city schools. TIC serves as a technology purchasing, repair and loan center for the Copenhagen schools. There are several classrooms used for short courses. Each teaching room is equipped with both a computer workstation station area with 15 computers and a discussion area.

The Open Computer Workshop is equipped with twenty computer workstations, printers and peripherals, and support staff are available in the lab to assist the users. TIC houses a graphic service center which assists institutions within the municipality with the production of printed materials. The center also provides space for student representatives from local schools to meet to produce a student news sheet. There are two rooms, with staff, devoted to technology support and training for business and industry. This service is provided to businesses on a for fee basis.

The information technology library is a specialized branch of the Copenhagen library system and works in cooperation with TIC. Occupying 150 m² on the first floor of the building, it has a separate entrance. It loans books, magazines, public domain software and manuals. The library has a

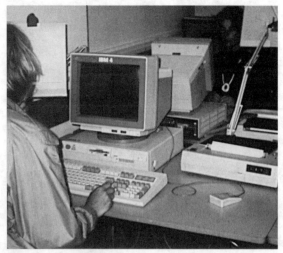

TIC provides public school teachers with training to learn computer applications and teach with them in the classroom.

Software library provides access to public domain software.

reception/information desk, an open access resource material area, a reading area, a work area with seven computer workstations, and an office. It is equipped with IBM and Macintosh computers and has CD-ROM resources. The library is staffed by two librarians and as many as five part-time assistants. It is open to the public five days a week.

Key Points

- TIC represents and early response to the need for a specialized facility to support the use of IT in schools.

- TIC supports IT in the curriculum through technical support; purchasing, distribution and repair of equipment; development of educational software and multimedia applications; and teacher training at the center and in the schools.

- TIC is the result of cooperation between the education, employment and library departments of the city government.

- The center provides a model for the renovation and reuse of older school buildings.

Reference

"Ungdomskultur: København i udvikling," internal publication of the Teknologi-Og Informatikcenteret, n.d.

The architect, Philip Cox's rendering of the entrance court to the new main OTEN facility in Strathfield

Model photo of OTEN's "purpose built" main facility, presently under construction

OTEN–The Open Training and Education Network

New South Wales, Australia

The increasing role of distance learning holds significant implications for education facilities. New methods of delivery promise changing patterns of use of existing facilities as well as the creation of new types of buildings. In particular, distance learning methods require the existence of production centers with professional staffing.

Through the Open Training and Education Network (OTEN), the government of New South Wales has developed a model of distance education that recognizes the importance distance learning delivery methods and the growing importance of information technology in education. Within the education structure of New South Wales, OTEN has taken distance learning, ". . . from being a backwater, in effect, the last option, . . . to being the first choice for many students."[1]

OTEN is organized as a central resource to support the New South Wales Vocational Technical and Further Education (NSW TAFE) system as well as schools and business. OTEN has built upon the organizational strength, established resources and student base available in the TAFE Colleges. OTEN is in the process of establishing Open Learning Centers as the focus of open and distance learning on each TAFE campus. The OLC's are physically integrated into the existing TAFE libraries to take advantage of established technological and resource platforms.

In the long term, OTEN's administrators see their programs enabling the Institutes to serve greater student enrollments at a marginal cost per student. Distance learning programs are expensive to operate in terms of facilities, equipment and transmission ($1500–2000 per hour for transponder time). By offering a centralized program through the Institutes and the schools, OTEN can realize the critical enrollment to make their programs cost effective.

By 1995 OTEN will occupy a new central facility on the site of the former Strathfield College of TAFE to accommodate the needs of OTEN's teaching and production staff, as well as the administrative, management and marketing functions. The new headquarters can be seen as a new type of educational facility, as can the Open Learning Centers designed to accommodate flexible patterns of use by students and staff.

The growing population of distance and open learning students will have implications for building use generally. These types of activities require greater open access to educational resources and fewer structured situations. The facilities that support distance and open learning students are study and work space, meeting rooms for tutorials, and facilities such as labs, libraries, studios, and rooms holding specialized equipment.

New Purpose-built headquarters
Opening 1995

Phillip Cox Richardson Taylor and Partners, Architects and Planners

EDUCATIONAL SERVICES

OTEN delivers a wide range of training and education programs available by distance education or flexible delivery. These services are targeted to learners in the public school system, TAFE colleges and the private sector. OTEN has developed a centralized model of distance education delivery in which a core of teaching and technical experts develop course materials and explore the use of technology for education delivery.

They also develop and evaluate innovative methods and technologies in education, including computer-assisted learning, multimedia, telecommunications and television broadcast technology. OTEN produces a variety of teaching, learning and training materials such as textbooks, videos, and computer-aided learning programs. For business, it offers a consultancy service for custom-designed workplace training programs.

Course materials and programs are distributed to students throughout the state. OTEN broadcasts live interactive courses via satellite to reception facilities located at TAFE Institutes throughout the state. The programs are further disseminated via videocassette tape and rebroadcasting. Students receive printed course materials in the mail for independent study with coordinated support services available at local TAFE Institutes. The institutes provide administrative and tutorial services, as well as the use of facilities, including the library and open learning center.

While OTEN is organized on functional lines, outlined below, a new structure will be in place prior to the move to Strathfield. The new structure will be based on a faculty model and will integrate the current functional areas into a more customer focussed organization. This structure will provide the new physical and organizational framework for the move to Strathfield.

- The **Open Learning Program** offers TAFE-accredited programs by distance delivery to over 23,000 students in all states of Australia and overseas. OTEN offers more than 120 TAFE major award courses.

- The **Education and Training Resource Centre** develops and produces learning materials for distance students, the TAFE Commission, TAFE Institutes and industry clients. ETRC also produces and delivers programs broadcast via satellite to students in TAFE Institutes and in secondary schools.

- Through the **Open High School** about 2900 public and private secondary school students study courses by distance methods.

- The **Learning Materials Production Centre** designs, develops and produces distance learning materials for schools from kindergarten to Year 12. The Media Production Unit develops and produces educational radio and television for school communities.

- The **Educational Technology and Communications** unit evaluates and develops new technologies in education including computer-assisted learning, multimedia, telecommunications and television broadcast technology. ET&C manages and supports the on-line library catalogue and produces and distributes the CD-ROM catalogue.

- **The Education Planning and Quality Assurance** unit manages educational planning activities evaluating student performance in OTEN courses and evaluating how well OTEN addresses issues of equity.

Mixed Mode Approach

OTEN supports a "mixed mode" approach of educational delivery as a highly effective method of distance learning. This means employing a combination of face-to-face instruction and self-study, including satellite broadcast, videotape, and printed course materials. Face to face sessions include tutorials, practical work assignments and assessment.

OTEN has found mixed-mode instruction to be a successful approach to distance education. In a trial program at Werrington College of TAFE students in mixed-mode courses did as well as those in face-to-face courses. Student satisfaction was high with an appreciation of the more autonomous approach to learning. Teachers also embraced the mixed mode approach to instruction. Local teachers valued being able to work with OTEN staff in implementing the program. Teachers expressed positive views toward the relaxed relationship with students, the high motivation of students, the use of tutorials to focus on student needs, and the ability to address issues of student access and equity.[3]

Building Design

In 1995 OTEN is scheduled to occupy a new, "purpose built," production and administrative center on the site of the former Strathfield College of TAFE. This building is designed as the main support facility for the distance and open learning programs in the state of New South Wales.

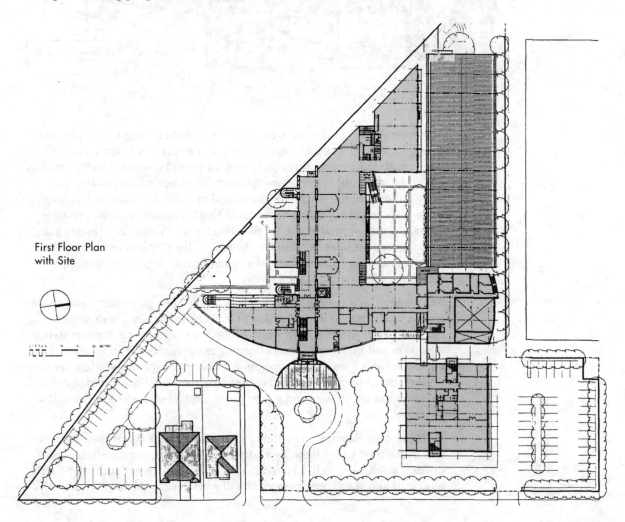

First Floor Plan
with Site

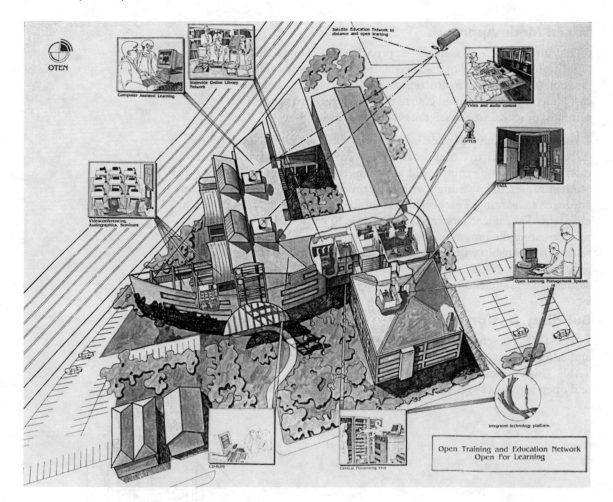

The design of the facility integrates two existing buildings with a series of three-story office wings to form a complex of structures around a central open courtyard. A new, three-story structure will be situated to the south as a buffer to the railway corridor adjacent to the site, and the existing one-story building to the north will allow light to reach the courtyard. A single-story entry pavilion leading to a double height circulation spine provides the main entry sequence and organization for the facility. A 25 meter high communications tower situated at the joint of the pavilion and circulation spine serves both a functional and a symbolic role, signaling the high-tech communications work of the facility.

The majority of the complex is programmed as open plan offices and space for the production and distribution of learning materials. These areas include a college administration unit, offices for teaching and support staff, a television and film studio, and a learning materials distribution center which includes a warehouse operation. Other areas include student services (information and counseling), three seminar rooms, a library/video center, an education technology and systems area, and a business center available for public hire.

OTEN will employ approximately 300 full-time and 300 part-time staff on-site. In addition to academic and administrative staff, graphic designers, desktop publishing staff, film/television producers, camera operators, technical staff and warehouse personnel will work within the facility. A small

Open Learning Center,
Taree College of TAFE

TAFE Library

Shared meeting Room

Open Learning Center

Satellite Reception/ Distance Learning Room

number of students will visit the site for tutorial support and use of the library. There will also be community access to the seminar rooms, library and business center.

This new facility will be the hub of a statewide system of TAFE Colleges and associated centers providing access points for flexible and open delivery of TAFE curricula. Learning materials will be developed in a wide range of media and distributed to students both directly and through the statewide system of access. This provision will be enhanced by a variety of teaching support strategies provided both directly by OTEN and through the local TAFE Colleges.

Open Learning Centers

Open Learning Centers (OLC) support "flexible delivery strategies" for technical and vocational education beyond the secondary level. OLC's are extensions of TAFE institute libraries. Open Learning students use the library's resources, and in turn the OLC provides satellite reception and video conferencing facilities for the college's use. When the library closes for the evening, the OLC remains open so students in the open and distance learning programs have access to equipment and resources 24 hours a day.

The OLC provides study space, access to computers and other technology including adaptive technology for students with disabilities, a multimedia platform to provide access to machine readable learning materials, and tutorial support, as well as satellite broadcast reception. Office space for OTEN staff is also provided in the OLC.

The role of the Open Learning Center:

- provide a focus for open learning,
- facilitate transfer of open learning techniques, educational technology and flexible delivery throughout NSW TAFE,
- facilitate integration of flexible delivery into Institute programs,
- deliver a wider number of course options to students and clients,
- provide 24 hour access to open learning resources,
- provide study space,
- provide space for tutorial support,
- provide educational video conferencing facilities..

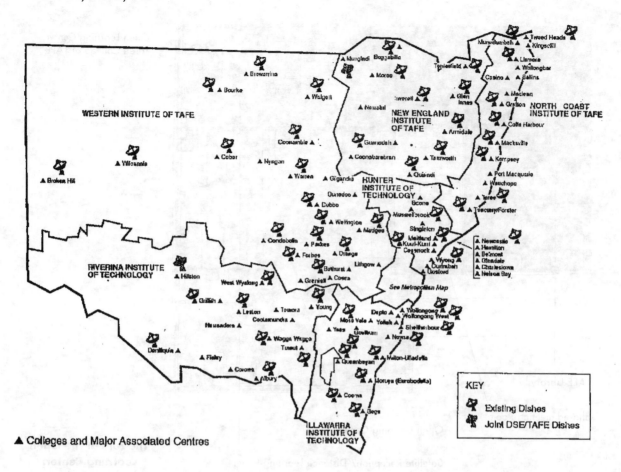

WESTERN INSTITUTE OF TAFE

NEW ENGLAND INSTITUTE OF TAFE

NORTH COAST INSTITUTE OF TAFE

HUNTER INSTITUTE OF TECHNOLOGY

RIVERINA INSTITUTE OF TECHNOLOGY

See Metropolitan Map

ILLAWARRA INSTITUTE OF TECHNOLOGY

KEY

▲ Colleges and Major Associated Centres

Existing Dishes

Joint DSE/TAFE Dishes

New South Wales has established satellite receiving stations at educational sites throughout the state.

OTEN's intention is to establish an OLC in each TAFE Institute. Presently the Australian government has funded the implementation of eleven OLC's at a cost of just under A$2 million and it is anticipated that more will be funded. The first group are all expected to be in service by 1995. In the future, all new TAFE library facilities will include an OLC as part of the plan.

Satellite Education and Training

The Open Training and Education Network was established ". . . to investigate and evaluate new and emerging technologies for educational delivery focusing particularly on those technologies which have an application to distance and flexible delivery."[4] The Satellite Education Service delivers education and training programs via satellite, reaching more than 90 TAFE colleges with satellite reception equipment. Programs have covered a variety of subject areas including computer training, retail customer contact skills, management training, real estate seminars and accounting. Live interactive programs that have been delivered include: short courses, skill upgrades, staff development, management information, new technology updates, panel discussions and seminars.

Live interactive programs operate with students at the receiving site viewing the satellite broadcast on a monitor and responding to the instructor via a toll-free telephone connection. The telephone transmissions are relayed directly to the instructor who addresses the issues raised and solves problems on the air. The Open Training and Education Network currently broadcasts uncoded signals so that anyone with the equipment can receive its programming. Only those students who register, however, receive support, evaluation and credit.

OTEN has provided custom designed courses direct to business and industry through a number of private satellite networks. These networks contract OTEN to produce television training courses which are then delivered to that network. This cooperative arrangement enables OTEN to make its unique expertise available more widely and has benefits for the business clients. OTEN is able to use some of the material it develops for the public education side of its operations, thus benefiting its larger, public client base through its private work.

KEY POINTS

- OTEN has statewide responsibility for the delivery of open and distance learning in New South Wales.

- OTEN's centralized model of education delivery through colleges and schools allows a critical mass of students to be reached, making programs cost-effective.

- OTEN produces a variety of teaching, learning and training materials.

- Open Learning Centers on TAFE College campuses are the focus of Distance and Open Learning and programs.

- OTEN supports a "mixed mode" approach to educational delivery.

- The Satellite Education and Training Network provides distance education programming.

- OTEN will occupy a new, "purpose-built" main facility in 1995.

REFERENCES

[1] Dagmar Schmidmaier, "The Client Focus in OTEN: Shaping an Organisation for Quality, Access and Service," OTEN, June 1993, p. 3.

[2] Dagmar Schmidmaier, *Introducing OTEN*, Open Training and Education Network, (NSW TAFE Commission, 1993), p. 1.

[3] Carole Lawson, "Report on Mixed Mode Delivery Trial in Advanced Certificate in Urban Horticulture at Werrington College of TAFE, Western Sydney Institute," OTEN, July, 1993.

[4] Dagmar Schmidmaier, Introduction to *Satellite Education and Training Network in the NSW TAFE Commission,* by Graeme Dobbs, Open Training and Education Network Occasional Papers 6, (NSW TAFE Commission, 1993), p. iii.

Glossary of Terms

10Base-T, IEEE standard for 10 Mbps Ethernet using unshielded twisted-pair cable. 10Base-T is configured in a star topology and has a maximum cable length of 325 feet per segment.

100Base-X, A "near Ethernet" scheme for transmitting at 100 Mbps over Ethernet-like media. This is one of a number of proposals currently under scrutiny by the networking community to upgrade speeds to desktop workstations.

AppleTalk, a local area network (LAN) protocol developed by Apple Computers Inc. to connect computers and peripherals.

ATM (Asynchronous Transfer Mode), part of the Broadband ISDN protocols, ATM is based upon a fixed size, 58 byte "cell." It is capable of very high speed switching of multimedia data streams.

Axonometric, a measured, three-dimensional drawing often used by architects to show a buildings massing or other spatial characteristics.

bandwidth, the range of frequencies in a band; the amount of information that can flow through a given point at a given time.

bit (b), a single unit of information; a binary unit.

bps, "bits per second," a basic measure of data transfer speed.

bridge, a device that connects two network segments using the same medium. Bridges operate at Level Two of the ISO model (the data layer) and are protocol sensitive.

bus, one or more conductors used for transmitting signals or power.

byte (B), a unit of information, eight bits.

cable trays, metal trays usually placed overhead, above the ceiling level, to carry electrical conduit and data networking cable.

casework, cabinets, shelves, desks, etc. designed for a particular space and application.

CD ROM (Compact Disc: Read Only Memory), a high-density information storage device. It uses light to read or write information in a digital form onto a disc.

clerestory windows, windows set above head height used to let natural light into a space.

coaxial cable, a cable that is used for data transfer. It consists of a central wire held within an insulator and a protective membrane.

CODEC, (coder-decoder) a device that transforms analog data into a digital bit stream (coder), and digital signals into analog data (decoder).

CPU (Central Processing Unit), the computer chip that directs all of the actions of the various parts of a computer.

digital, encoding of information into binary code; all data is represented by a combination of ones and zeros.

distance learning, a general term used to describe a variety of educational arrangements by which a student is enrolled in an accredited course or school but completes the educational requirements without having to attend class at the school. Communication is achieved through a variety of means, including telephone, mail, E-mail, cable television and satellite broadcast.

downlink, the ability to receive satellite broadcasts. C and Ku are two common satellite signal types or "bands."

dynamic allocation of network addresses, the ability to negotiate an unused address among peers operating on a network. AppleTalk is an example of a dynamic allocation protocol.

EIA (Electronic Industries Association), an association that sets communications standards for the telecommunications industry.

EMI (Electromagnetic Interference), the emitted radiation of any piece of electromechanical hardware that interferes with the normal transmission of some other hardware.

energy pillars, a column, or vertical conduit, designed for use in the Tilburg University library through which power and network cabling are supplied to desktops anywhere in the library.

Ethernet, a local area network protocol developed by the Xerox Corporation. Ethernet networks use Carrier-Sense Multiple Access with Collision Detection (CSMA/CD), transmitting at 10 Mbps. IEEE standard 802.3 is similar to Ethernet.

extensible, capable of being extended; most often used to indicate that a given solution will work over small to large problem sets.

FDDI (Fiber Distributed Data Interface), a standard established by the American National Standards Institute (ANSI) for transmissions over fiber optic media.

fileserver, a computer that stores information for use by other computers on a network.

flat-panel displays, thin, low-powered display devices. Liquid crystal (used extensively in laptop and notebook computer displays) and plasma displays are examples of flat-panel devices.

FPS (Frames Per Second), the rate at which video images are transferred to the display screen.

full-motion video, transmission and display of visual images at rate a which simulates the appearance of full-motion. NTSC and Pal broadcast video standards are examples.

Gopher, an information retrieval system created at the University of Minnesota. In wide use on the Internet.

graphical user interface, a "user interface" (the manner by which the user and the computer communicate information) that is based on icons,

pointer devices (such as a mouse, trackball or pen) and a mixture of text, images and possibly even motion and sound (though motion and sound are more often referred to as multimedia).

hard-wired, a direct wiring connection, without the ability to disconnect, i.e. there is no "plug" or "socket."

head end, a term commonly used within the cable television industry to denote the location of the main communications hub for a facility, or campus, containing reception and switching equipment, as well as recording devices and other equipment related to the management of a telecommunications network.

hertz (Hz), a unit of frequency, equal to one cycle per second.

host, an entity that has an address on the network; remote devices use the host address to access the host.

hub, a modern multiport repeater--a device that allows multiple transmission media types (twisted pair, thin and thick coaxial cable, and fiber optic cable) to be connected together to form a single network at the media level. (See also **Star Topology**.)

IEEE (Institute of Electrical and Electronic Engineers), a professional society responsible for defining many commonly used standards.

interface, the physical connection of more than one piece of equipment or of a network; the procedural connection, such as a protocol, that enables separate pieces of equipment to interact.

Internet, a network of regional, national and governmental networks in over 35 countries.

interstitial, pertaining to, situated in or forming a small or narrow space or interval between things or parts.

IP (Internet Protocol), a telecommunications protocol used on the Internet.

IPX, the ISO layer three protocol used by Novell NetWare.

ISDN, a proprietary digital information network developed by AT&T.

ISO layer, any of seven levels in a model proposed by the International Standards Organization (ISO) to describe the functions and relationships in computer networks. The lowest layers (one and two) specify media standards; upper layers specify functions more visible to users and programs using the network.

LAN (Local Area Network), a network that connects hosts within a limited area, usually consisting of Ethernet cable, baseband cable, broadband cable or token rings.

microprocessor, a chip or integrated circuit, that executes an instruction set.

modem, (modulator-demodulator) a device that translates digital signals from a computer into analog signals for transmission, used for transmission over telephone lines.

multicast video, a suite of protocols using *multicasting* to permit computers to join, or leave, video conferences. *Multicast* is a networking scheme by which computers dynamically "join" and "leave" groups.

multimedia, the integrated use of "rich" text (e.g. bold, italic, different fonts), images and sounds to communicate information.

network, a cabling system by which two or more computers are directly linked to each other.

node, the point of intersection of more than one network cable; also, the piece of equipment at that intersection.

noise, the presence of electromagnetic interference extraneous to the intended signal.

non-reusable password technology, small, typically credit-card sized, devices used to generate passwords for entry systems.

Novell server, a proprietary operating system developed and maintained by the Novell Corporation.

operating system, the specific software that controls the execution of programs, provides shared access to devices and ensures the integrity of resources, e.g. memory, disks.

optical disk, a high-density data storage medium that uses light to encode and read information.

optical fiber, a thin filament of glass or other transparent material through which a signal-encoded light beam may be transmitted.

peripherals, electronic components attached to a computer station to supplement or expand its storage or graphic capacity, i.e. external drives, CD ROM drives, Video camera, scanner, etc.

pixel (picture element), the smallest unit of display, a phosphor on a video screen or a "dot" on a printout.

port, a physical access point of a computer or network.

protocol, the language or actions used to exchange information among computers and other hosts.

RAM (Random Access Memory), a chip-based storage medium into which data can quickly be written and read. If electric power is lost, the information is lost.

relevance feedback, a methods used by (WAIS) to find more documents like the previous one.

remote connectivity, the ability for a remote site (such as a home or remote office) to appear as if it is directly connected to a business's network. Apple Remote Access (ARA), the Point to Point Protocol (PPP) and Serial Line Internet Protocol (SLIP) are examples of protocols that allow a remote user to have the same network view as directly connected users.

repeater, a device that regenerates and retimes a digital data signal in order to extend its physical range.

ring topology, a local area network topology in which all nodes are connected in a closed loop.

RISC (Reduced Instruction Set Computing), a microprocessor that deals with a reduced set of operating instructions; intended to speed operations.

ROM (Read Only Memory), a non-volatile chip based memory storage device whose contents cannot be written over.

router, a device that can interconnect networks over long-distances and usually over different media. Routers operate at level three of the ISO model (the network layer) and are protocol sensitive.

SCSI (Small Computer Systems Interface); pronounced "scuzzy"; defines a set of standards for the connection of computers to peripherals such as hard disks, CD ROM drives, etc.

serial interface, an interface in which bits are sent sequentially.

shielded twisted-pair (STP), a pair of wires twisted together and covered with a conductive material to provide any potentially produced noise a quick path to the ground.

star topology, a network which has all nodes connected together through a single, central node.

TCP/IP protocol stack, a collection of telecommunications programs associated with the Transmission Control Protocol (TCP) and the Internet Protocol (IP), including telnet, FTP, SMTP, DNS, TFTP, BOOTP, SNMP, NFS, RPC, TCP UDP, ICMP, IGMP, RIP, BGP, ARP, RARP, etc.

telecommunications riser, a vertical conduit or shaft used to run cabling from floor to floor within a building.

thin Ethernet, the common term for IEEE specification 802.3 Type 10 Base-2 which uses RG58 coaxial cable for transmission of Ethernet formatted data.

token ring, IEEE specification 802.5 for connecting a set of stations to some transmission medium. A station puts a message onto the ring, each station, including the recipient, in turn copies the message. When the original sender receives its message back, it deletes the message from the ring.

topology, the configuration that defines the relationship between nodes in a network; see **star topology**, **ring topology**.

touch-screen technology, the ability to make selections and control computer processes by touching highlighted areas on a computer monitor.

transceiver, a piece of hardware that allows a computer's signal to be transmitted and received within a given transmission medium.

trunk, all of the cable segments and related hardware of a cable network.

unshielded twisted-pair (UTP), a cable typically constructed of multiple pairs of twisted wires that are unshielded in a PVC or plenum-rated sheath. UTP cable is commonly associated with 10Base-T networks.

uplink, to transmit a signal to a satellite for broadcast.

video capture, the ability to digitize a full motion video signal and store it in a computer.

video compression technology, the use of mathematical algorithms to reduce the size of digital information for transmission.

WAIS (wide area information servers), a set of databases containing information on thousands of topics. The WAIS protocol includes tools to search these databases using natural language queries and provides relevance feedback for refining the search process.

WAN (wide-area network), a WAN includes long-distance communications, such as long-distance telephone circuits, fiber optic cable or satellite media. Often composed of LANs, a WAN can integrate WANs and LANs.

wiring closet, the physical location through which a building's wiring is routed; serves as a termination point for wiring.

Bibliography

Alexander, Christopher. *A Pattern Language*. New York: Oxford University Press, 1977.

Beare, H. and R. Slaughter. *Education for the Twenty-first Century*. (London: Routledge) 1993.

Clarkson, Austin, and Karen Pegely. "An Assessment of a Technology in Music Programme: Research Summary", The Centre for the Study of Computers in Education at York University North York, Ontario, June 1991.

Clarkson, Austin, Jerome Durlak and Karen Pegely. "Creative Applications for Multi-Sensory Interactive Media: Research Summary", The Centre for the Study of Computers in Education at York University North York, Ontario, December 1992.

Cruickshank and Seward, Architects. Brief on Oldham Sixth Form College, Manchester England.

Cuban, Larry. *Teachers and Machines: The Classroom Use of Technology Since 1920. Teachers College Press*, Teachers College, Columbia University, New York City, New York, 1988.

Daryl Jackson Pty. Ltd., Architects. *Methodist Ladies' College: 1992 Masterplan. "Executive Summary." Section 1.6.*

"Directed Study." Lester B. Pearson High School: A New Vision of Education for the Year 2000. School handout.

Dobbs, Graeme. Satellite Education and Training *Network in the NSW TAFE Commission*, Open Training and Education Network Occasional Papers 6, (NSW TAFE Commission, 1993).

Durlak, Jerome, T. "The Use of Interactive Media in a Creative Applications Programme: A Pilot Study", The Centre for the Study of Computers in Education at York University North York, Ontario, February 1992.

Dwyer, D. C Ringstaff, and J. Sandholtz. "Trading Places: When Teachers Utilize Students' Expertise in Technology -Intensive Classrooms." Paper presented at the annual meeting of the American Educational Research Association, Chicago, IL. 1991.

Dwyer, D., Ringstaff, C. and Sandholtz, J. "The Evolution of Teachers' Instructional Beliefs and Practices in High-Access-to-Technology Classrooms". Paper presented at the annual meeting of the American Educational Research Association, Boston, MA., 1990.;

Enders, Alexandra and Marian Hall, Editors. *The Assistive Technology Source Book*, Resna Press, Washington, D.C. 1990

Farley, Raymond P. "Classrooms of the Future." *The American School Board Journal*. March 1993, Vol. 180, No. 3. p. 32-34.

Fayes, James. "Brief on Campus 2000", European Studies Program, Ulster Folk and Transport Museum, North Ireland.

Grasso, Irene and Margaret Fallshaw, eds. Reflections of a Leaning Community: Views on the Introduction of Laptops at MLC, (Victoria, Australia: Ladies Methodist College), 1993.

Hein, Hilde. *The Exploratorium: The Museum as Laboratory*, Smithsonian Institution Press, Washington, D.C., 1990.

Koster, Guy. "Synopsis of network installation and infrastructure installed by AEC on behalf of Oldham Metropolitan Borough Council at the Oldham Sixth Form College." AEC, 1994.

Lawson, Carole. "Report on Mixed Mode Delivery Trial in Advanced Certificate in Urban Horticulture at Werrington College of TAFE, Western Sydney Institute," OTEN, July, 1993.

Leino, Jarkko. Innovative School: Knowledge as a Dynamic Concept, University of Tampere, Finland.

Longhurst, Brian. "Distance Learning Report of a Phase I Study", Salford University, British Telecom, 1992.

Morris, Lori V. and Drew Gitomer. "The Final Report of the Formative Evaluation of Hunterdon Central Regional High School's Reform Effort in a Technological Environment." Educational Testing Service: Princeton, NJ, August 1, 1993.

Moyal, Ann Mozley. *Clear Across Australia.: A History of Telecommunications*, Melbourne, Victoria: Nelson, 1984.

Nakayama, Kazuhiko. "How to Maintain Human Inter-action and Individualized Learning in a Large Class-room with Microcomputer - Based CAI", Educational Executive Conference, Singapore, 17-19 August 1988.

Owston, D., Sharon Murphy and Herbert Wideman. "On and Off computer Writing of Eighth Grade Students Experienced in Word Processing: Research Summary", The Centre for the Study of Computers in Education at York University North York, Ontario, May 1990.

Papert, Seymour. *The Children's Machine: Rethinking School in the Age of the Computer*, New York: Basic Books, c. 1993.

Pelgrum, William and Tjeerd Plomp. *The Use of Computers in Education Worldwide*, IEA, Oxford:Pergamon Press, 1991;

Pelgrum, William I.A.M., Janssen Reine and Tjeerd Plomp, *Schools, Teachers, Students and Computers: A Cross-National Perspective*, International Association for the Evaluation of Educational Achievement, 1993.

PEB Exchange, No 21, OECD, Paris February 1994.

"Portables: Choosing and using portable computers." National Council for Educational Technology: Coventry, England 1992.

"Portables: Portable computers in Initial Teacher Education." National Council for Educational Technology: Coventry, England 1993.

Prospectus 1993/94: Choice • Opportunity • Culture. Oldham Education Authority, 1993.

"Prototype Classrooms Catapult Learning into the 21st Century." *Hunterdon Central Digest.* Summer 1993, p.1-3.

Rask, Sauli. "The Kuokkala School Project." AERA Annual Meeting. April 20-24. 1993.

Ryan, Tony. "Greenfield Site to Open Learning." Adult Education News: Newsletter of the Australian Association of Adult and Community Education. Australian Post: Publication no. NBH 0921, July 1992.

Sachsse, Michael. "Open Learning: Its Implication for Students and Teachers." Post Compulsory Education 93 Directions Conference. Perth, Australia, November, 21-23, 1993.

Safra, Martine. "The Educational Infrastructure on Rural Areas", OECD Paris 1994.

Schement, Jorge Reina. "Beyond Universal Service: Characteristics of Americans without Telephones, 1980-1993, Communications Policy Working Paper 1," Benton Foundation, Washington, D.C., 1994., Universal Service and the Information Highway, Communications Policy Briefing 1, Benton Foundation, Washington, D.C., 1994.

Schmidmaier, Dagmar. "The Client Focus in OTEN: Shaping an Organisation for Quality, Access and Service," OTEN, June 1993.

Schmidmaier, Dagmar. "Introduction to Satellite Education and Training Network in the NSW TAFE Commission," by Graeme Dobbs, Open Training and Education Network Occasional Papers 6, (NSW TAFE Commission, 1993).

Sheingold, Karen. *Restructuring for Learning With Technology*, Center for Technology in Education, Bank Street College and the National Center on Education and the Economy, New York, NY..

Shipp, Heather. "The Marshmead Curriculum." *The Star*. [Quarterly magazine published for the MLC community.] Vol. 6, No. 4. 1992.

Smith, Gerry. " Restructuring Education at River Oaks P.S.: A Vision for the Future", draft paper, June 1993, p.

Stuebing, S. *Campus, Classroom, Connections*, Newark, New Jersey: New Jersey Institute of Technology, 1994.

Stuebing, S., *School Design Notebook*, New Jersey Institute of Technology, Newark, New Jersey, 1992, Case Study #16.

"Technology Across The Curriculum At Adelaide's School of the Future",Arts and Education, Australia, November 1993.

"The Teaching and Learning of Information Technology", Department of Education and Science, London, England, 1991.

Thompson, Andy, et al. *Educational Design Initiatives in City Technology Colleges. Building Bulletin 72* The Department of Education and Science, London, England, 1991.

Tilburg University. The University Library of the Future Today. Tilburg: Tilburg University Press, 1992

Turnbull, Graham. "The Laptop Project: Interim Report." The Scottish Council for Educational Technology: Glasgow, 1991.

Update 3: Our New College. From Vision to Reality. Oldham Education Authority, Autumn 1992.

Watson, Deryn. *The Impact Summary: An Evaluation of The Impact of Information Technology on Children's Achievements in Primary and Secondary Schools*, Department for Education, Kings College, London, England, 1993.

Willis, Norman. "New Technology and Its Impact on Educational Buildings", Paris: Programme on Educational Buildings, Organisation for Economic Co-operation and Development, 1992.

About The Research Team

SUSAN STUEBING, Assistant Professor for Research

Prof. Stuebing, a Registered Architect, directs the research in learning environments at Architecture and Building Science (ABS) at the New Jersey Institute of Technology (NJIT). She has conducted research with educational and public organizations including: Apple Computers Apple Classrooms of Tomorrow Project (ACOT); the American Federation of Teachers; the National Governors' Association, the New Jersey Commission for Business Efficiency in the Public Schools; and local school districts in New Jersey including Hudson, Bergen, Hunterdon and Morris Counties as well as school districts throughout the United States. In addition to the New Jersey Institute of Technology, Prof. Stuebing has taught Architecture at Roger Williams College, and Tufts University. She has more than 15 years experience as a planner and an architect. She received her MArch. Degree from the Massachusetts Institute of Technology and her B.B.A. (General Finance and Urban Management) from the University of Massachusetts in Amherst, Massachusetts. She is principle author of *Campus, Classrooms, Connections* and *The School Design Notebook*, both published by the New Jersey Institute of Technology.

Architectural Researchers

ANTON WOLFSHORNDL

Mr. Wolfshorndl has conducted research in educational environments at ABS for the past three years. He received an MArch Degree from the School of Architecture at NJIT. Mr. Wolfshorndl was awarded the Henry Adams Certificate of Merit for Excellence in the Study of Architecture from the American Institute of Architects (AIA) and an Honorable Mention for Excellence in Design from the School of Architecture. Prior to his work in the field of architecture, he received his M.A. in American Literature and taught English as an adjunct professor at several New Jersey colleges. Mr. Wolfshorndl was Project Manager for *Campus, Classrooms, Connections* and a member of the research team for *The School Design Notebook*.

STEPHANIE E. DIPETRILLO

Ms. DiPetrillo received a Master of Architecture degree from the School of Architecture at NJIT. While at NJIT, Ms. DiPetrillo was awarded the Excellence in Teaching Award. She holds a B.A. in Economics from Rutgers College. Her past research includes documentation of historical buildings and structures.

LESLIE KNOX COUSINEAU

Ms. Cousineau is currently the Executive Director at The Chicago Institute for the Study Of Architecture and Technology. With the Education Team at ABS, Ms. Cousineau researched technology-rich learning environments from 1990-1993. Ms. Cousineau received her MArch degree from the School of Architecture at NJIT. She was awarded the School of Architecture Medal for overall excellence and received an AIA Scholarship.

MAIN SALES OUTLETS OF OECD PUBLICATIONS
PRINCIPAUX POINTS DE VENTE DES PUBLICATIONS DE L'OCDE

ARGENTINA – ARGENTINE
Carlos Hirsch S.R.L.
Galería Güemes, Florida 165, 4° Piso
1333 Buenos Aires   Tel. (1) 331.1787 y 331.2391
Telefax: (1) 331.1787

AUSTRALIA – AUSTRALIE
D.A. Information Services
648 Whitehorse Road, P.O.B 163
Mitcham, Victoria 3132   Tel. (03) 873.4411
Telefax: (03) 873.5679

AUSTRIA – AUTRICHE
Gerold & Co.
Graben 31
Wien I   Tel. (0222) 533.50.14
Telefax: (0222) 512.47.31.29

BELGIUM – BELGIQUE
Jean De Lannoy
Avenue du Roi 202
B-1060 Bruxelles   Tel. (02) 538.51.69/538.08.41
Telefax: (02) 538.08.41

CANADA
Renouf Publishing Company Ltd.
1294 Algoma Road
Ottawa, ON K1B 3W8   Tel. (613) 741.4333
Telefax: (613) 741.5439
Stores:
61 Sparks Street
Ottawa, ON K1P 5R1   Tel. (613) 238.8985
211 Yonge Street
Toronto, ON M5B 1M4   Tel. (416) 363.3171
Telefax: (416)363.59.63

Les Éditions La Liberté Inc.
3020 Chemin Sainte-Foy
Sainte-Foy, PQ G1X 3V6   Tel. (418) 658.3763
Telefax: (418) 658.3763

Federal Publications Inc.
165 University Avenue, Suite 701
Toronto, ON M5H 3B8   Tel. (416) 860.1611
Telefax: (416) 860.1608

Les Publications Fédérales
1185 Université
Montréal, QC H3B 3A7   Tel. (514) 954.1633
Telefax: (514) 954.1635

CHINA – CHINE
China National Publications Import
Export Corporation (CNPIEC)
16 Gongti E. Road, Chaoyang District
P.O. Box 88 or 50
Beijing 100704 PR   Tel. (01) 506.6688
Telefax: (01) 506.3101

CHINESE TAIPEI – TAIPEI CHINOIS
Good Faith Worldwide Int'l. Co. Ltd.
9th Floor, No. 118, Sec. 2
Chung Hsiao E. Road
Taipei   Tel. (02) 391.7396/391.7397
Telefax: (02) 394.9176

**CZECH REPUBLIC – RÉPUBLIQUE
TCHÈQUE**
Artia Pegas Press Ltd.
Narodni Trida 25
POB 825
111 21 Praha 1   Tel. 26.65.68
Telefax: 26.20.81

DENMARK – DANEMARK
Munksgaard Book and Subscription Service
35, Nørre Søgade, P.O. Box 2148
DK-1016 København K   Tel. (33) 12.85.70
Telefax: (33) 12.93.87

EGYPT – ÉGYPTE
Middle East Observer
41 Sherif Street
Cairo   Tel. 392.6919
Telefax: 360-6804

FINLAND – FINLANDE
Akateeminen Kirjakauppa
Keskuskatu 1, P.O. Box 128
00100 Helsinki
Subscription Services/Agence d'abonnements :
P.O. Box 23
00371 Helsinki   Tel. (358 0) 12141
Telefax: (358 0) 121.4450

FRANCE
OECD/OCDE
Mail Orders/Commandes par correspondance:
2, rue André-Pascal
75775 Paris Cedex 16   Tel. (33-1) 45.24.82.00
Telefax: (33-1) 49.10.42.76
Telex: 640048 OCDE

Orders via Minitel, France only/
Commandes par Minitel, France exclusivement :
36 15 OCDE

OECD Bookshop/Librairie de l'OCDE :
33, rue Octave-Feuillet
75016 Paris   Tel. (33-1) 45.24.81.81
(33-1) 45.24.81.67

Documentation Française
29, quai Voltaire
75007 Paris   Tel. 40.15.70.00

Gibert Jeune (Droit-Économie)
6, place Saint-Michel
75006 Paris   Tel. 43.25.91.19

Librairie du Commerce International
10, avenue d'Iéna
75016 Paris   Tel. 40.73.34.60

Librairie Dunod
Université Paris-Dauphine
Place du Maréchal de Lattre de Tassigny
75016 Paris   Tel. (1) 44.05.40.13

Librairie Lavoisier
11, rue Lavoisier
75008 Paris   Tel. 42.65.39.95

Librairie L.G.D.J. - Montchrestien
20, rue Soufflot
75005 Paris   Tel. 46.33.89.85

Librairie des Sciences Politiques
30, rue Saint-Guillaume
75007 Paris   Tel. 45.48.36.02

P.U.F.
49, boulevard Saint-Michel
75005 Paris   Tel. 43.25.83.40

Librairie de l'Université
12a, rue Nazareth
13100 Aix-en-Provence   Tel. (16) 42.26.18.08

Documentation Française
165, rue Garibaldi
69003 Lyon   Tel. (16) 78.63.32.23

Librairie Decitre
29, place Bellecour
69002 Lyon   Tel. (16) 72.40.54.54

Librairie Sauramps
Le Triangle
34967 Montpellier Cedex 2   Tel. (16) 67.58.85.15
Tekefax: (16) 67.58.27.36

GERMANY – ALLEMAGNE
OECD Publications and Information Centre
August-Bebel-Allee 6
D-53175 Bonn   Tel. (0228) 959.120
Telefax: (0228) 959.12.17

GREECE – GRÈCE
Librairie Kauffmann
Mavrokordatou 9
106 78 Athens   Tel. (01) 32.55.321
Telefax: (01) 32.30.320

HONG-KONG
Swindon Book Co. Ltd.
Astoria Bldg. 3F
34 Ashley Road, Tsimshatsui
Kowloon, Hong Kong   Tel. 2376.2062
Telefax: 2376.0685

HUNGARY – HONGRIE
Euro Info Service
Margitsziget, Európa Ház
1138 Budapest   Tel. (1) 111.62.16
Telefax: (1) 111.60.61

ICELAND – ISLANDE
Mál Mog Menning
Laugavegi 18, Pósthólf 392
121 Reykjavik   Tel. (1) 552.4240
Telefax: (1) 562.3523

INDIA – INDE
Oxford Book and Stationery Co.
Scindia House
New Delhi 110001   Tel. (11) 331.5896/5308
Telefax: (11) 332.5993

17 Park Street
Calcutta 700016   Tel. 240832

INDONESIA – INDONÉSIE
Pdii-Lipi
P.O. Box 4298
Jakarta 12042   Tel. (21) 573.34.67
Telefax: (21) 573.34.67

IRELAND – IRLANDE
Government Supplies Agency
Publications Section
4/5 Harcourt Road
Dublin 2   Tel. 661.31.11
Telefax: 475.27.60

ISRAEL
Praedicta
5 Shatner Street
P.O. Box 34030
Jerusalem 91430   Tel. (2) 52.84.90/1/2
Telefax: (2) 52.84.93

R.O.Y. International
P.O. Box 13056
Tel Aviv 61130   Tel. (3) 49.61.08
Telefax: (3) 544.60.39

Palestinian Authority/Middle East:
INDEX Information Services
P.O.B. 19502
Jerusalem   Tel. (2) 27.12.19
Telefax: (2) 27.16.34

ITALY – ITALIE
Libreria Commissionaria Sansoni
Via Duca di Calabria 1/1
50125 Firenze   Tel. (055) 64.54.15
Telefax: (055) 64.12.57

Via Bartolini 29
20155 Milano   Tel. (02) 36.50.83

Editrice e Libreria Herder
Piazza Montecitorio 120
00186 Roma   Tel. 679.46.28
Telefax: 678.47.51

Libreria Hoepli
Via Hoepli 5
20121 Milano   Tel. (02) 86.54.46
Telefax: (02) 805.28.86

Libreria Scientifica
Dott. Lucio de Biasio 'Aeiou'
Via Coronelli, 6
20146 Milano   Tel. (02) 48.95.45.52
Telefax: (02) 48.95.45.48

JAPAN – JAPON
OECD Publications and Information Centre
Landic Akasaka Building
2-3-4 Akasaka, Minato-ku
Tokyo 107   Tel. (81.3) 3586.2016
Telefax: (81.3) 3584.7929

KOREA – CORÉE
Kyobo Book Centre Co. Ltd.
P.O. Box 1658, Kwang Hwa Moon
Seoul   Tel. 730.78.91
Telefax: 735.00.30

MALAYSIA – MALAISIE
University of Malaya Bookshop
University of Malaya
P.O. Box 1127, Jalan Pantai Baru
59700 Kuala Lumpur
Malaysia   Tel. 756.5000/756.5425
                            Telefax: 756.3246

MEXICO – MEXIQUE
Revistas y Periodicos Internacionales S.A. de C.V.
Florencia 57 - 1004
Mexico, D.F. 06600   Tel. 207.81.00
                           Telefax: 208.39.79

NETHERLANDS – PAYS-BAS
SDU Uitgeverij Plantijnstraat
Externe Fondsen
Postbus 20014
2500 EA's-Gravenhage   Tel. (070) 37.89.880
Voor bestellingen: Telefax: (070) 34.75.778

**NEW ZEALAND
NOUVELLE-ZÉLANDE**
Legislation Services
P.O. Box 12418
Thorndon, Wellington   Tel. (04) 496.5652
                          Telefax: (04) 496.5698

NORWAY – NORVÈGE
Narvesen Info Center – NIC
Bertrand Narvesens vei 2
P.O. Box 6125 Etterstad
0602 Oslo 6   Tel. (022) 57.33.00
                          Telefax: (022) 68.19.01

PAKISTAN
Mirza Book Agency
65 Shahrah Quaid-E-Azam
Lahore 54000   Tel. (42) 353.601
                          Telefax: (42) 231.730

PHILIPPINE – PHILIPPINES
International Book Center
5th Floor, Filipinas Life Bldg.
Ayala Avenue
Metro Manila   Tel. 81.96.76
                        Telex 23312 RHP PH

PORTUGAL
Livraria Portugal
Rua do Carmo 70-74
Apart. 2681
1200 Lisboa   Tel. (01) 347.49.82/5
                          Telefax: (01) 347.02.64

SINGAPORE – SINGAPOUR
Gower Asia Pacific Pte Ltd.
Golden Wheel Building
41, Kallang Pudding Road, No. 04-03
Singapore 1334   Tel. 741.5166
                           Telefax: 742.9356

SPAIN – ESPAGNE
Mundi-Prensa Libros S.A.
Castelló 37, Apartado 1223
Madrid 28001   Tel. (91) 431.33.99
                          Telefax: (91) 575.39.98

Libreria Internacional AEDOS
Consejo de Ciento 391
08009 – Barcelona   Tel. (93) 488.30.09
                           Telefax: (93) 487.76.59

Llibreria de la Generalitat
Palau Moja
Rambla dels Estudis, 118
08002 – Barcelona
                    (Subscripcions) Tel. (93) 318.80.12
                    (Publicacions) Tel. (93) 302.67.23
                           Telefax: (93) 412.18.54

SRI LANKA
Centre for Policy Research
c/o Colombo Agencies Ltd.
No. 300-304, Galle Road
Colombo 3   Tel. (1) 574240, 573551-2
                       Telefax: (1) 575394, 510711

SWEDEN – SUÈDE
Fritzes Customer Service
S–106 47 Stockholm   Tel. (08) 690.90.90
                          Telefax: (08) 20.50.21

Subscription Agency/Agence d'abonnements :
Wennergren-Williams Info AB
P.O. Box 1305
171 25 Solna   Tel. (08) 705.97.50
                          Telefax: (08) 27.00.71

SWITZERLAND – SUISSE
Maditec S.A. (Books and Periodicals - Livres
et périodiques)
Chemin des Palettes 4
Case postale 266
1020 Renens VD 1   Tel. (021) 635.08.65
                          Telefax: (021) 635.07.80

Librairie Payot S.A.
4, place Pépinet
CP 3212
1002 Lausanne   Tel. (021) 341.33.47
                          Telefax: (021) 341.33.45

Librairie Unilivres
6, rue de Candolle
1205 Genève   Tel. (022) 320.26.23
                          Telefax: (022) 329.73.18

Subscription Agency/Agence d'abonnements :
Dynapresse Marketing S.A.
38 avenue Vibert
1227 Carouge   Tel. (022) 308.07.89
                          Telefax: (022) 308.07.99

See also – Voir aussi :
OECD Publications and Information Centre
August-Bebel-Allee 6
D-53175 Bonn (Germany)   Tel. (0228) 959.120
                          Telefax: (0228) 959.12.17

THAILAND – THAÏLANDE
Suksit Siam Co. Ltd.
113, 115 Fuang Nakhon Rd.
Opp. Wat Rajbopith
Bangkok 10200   Tel. (662) 225.9531/2
                           Telefax: (662) 222.5188

TURKEY – TURQUIE
Kültür Yayinlari Is-Türk Ltd. Sti.
Atatürk Bulvari No. 191/Kat 13
Kavaklidere/Ankara   Tel. 428.11.40 Ext. 2458
Dolmabahce Cad. No. 29
Besiktas/Istanbul   Tel. 260.71.88
                            Telex: 43482B

UNITED KINGDOM – ROYAUME-UNI
HMSO
Gen. enquiries   Tel. (071) 873 0011
Postal orders only:
P.O. Box 276, London SW8 5DT
Personal Callers HMSO Bookshop
49 High Holborn, London WC1V 6HB
                           Telefax: (071) 873 8200
Branches at: Belfast, Birmingham, Bristol,
Edinburgh, Manchester

UNITED STATES – ÉTATS-UNIS
OECD Publications and Information Center
2001 L Street N.W., Suite 650
Washington, D.C. 20036-4910 Tel. (202) 785.6323
                           Telefax: (202) 785.0350

VENEZUELA
Libreria del Este
Avda F. Miranda 52, Aptdo. 60337
Edificio Galipán
Caracas 106   Tel. 951.1705/951.2307/951.1297
                     Telegram: Libreste Caracas

Subscription to OECD periodicals may also be
placed through main subscription agencies.

Les abonnements aux publications périodiques de
l'OCDE peuvent être souscrits auprès des
principales agences d'abonnement.

Orders and inquiries from countries where Distribu-
tors have not yet been appointed should be sent to:
OECD Publications Service, 2 rue André-Pascal,
75775 Paris Cedex 16, France.

Les commandes provenant de pays où l'OCDE n'a
pas encore désigné de distributeur peuvent être
adressées à : OCDE, Service des Publications,
2, rue André-Pascal, 75775 Paris Cedex 16, France.

5-1995